# The Basic

# Ninja Foodi

## Air Fryer

## Cookbook for Beginners

### UK 2023

The Latest and Great Guide of Over 600 Healthy and Crispy Air Fryer Recipes
for Every Day Meals incl. Side Dishes, Desserts and More

## Kennith Schaden

# Table of Contents

## Chapter 6 Beef, Pork, and Lamb

## Chapter 7 Desserts

# INTRODUCTION

It's hard to beat the warm feeling of dining at a favourite restaurant, chewing on meat so tender and juicy. But what if you could prepare chef-quality prime beef at home and without all the fuss?

The Ninja Air Fryer reduces the guilt you would otherwise feel after spending pounds on a 5-star restaurant meal. It will make your food taste like it came from a gourmet chef —without all of the excess fat and grease.

We've been using the Ninja Air Fryer for a couple of months and we love it because our weeknight meals cravings are satisfied within a few minutes. It's easy to use and cleanup is so quick. The first recipe that we tried was the crispy chicken wings with honey mustard sauce and parmesan cheese dip. It turned out delicious. Also, whenever we feel like burgers are getting old—or our waistlines are expanding too much —we turn on our air fryer and take advantage of its many benefits: low-fat steaks in no time!

Ninja brought back life to our meal time because of its fat-free, quick and easy cooking. So we thought of sharing the same taste of our meals with this cookbook. It's the compilation of the best recipes you can cook in your Ninja Air Fryer and add variety to your everyday cooking. It has recipes for breakfast, lunch, and dinner (and desserts) so you won't get bored of eating the same routine food.

Whether you're a foodie looking to cook up different and unique meals or a beginner who wants simple recipes, this book will turn your next cookout into an all-you-can eat party. Vegetarians, fish lovers, meat-eaters and snack fanatics will all find recipes that appeal to them in this book. No matter what diet you follow—this cookbook has something for everyone!

Each recipe has simple ingredients that can be purchased at your local grocery store and is bound to taste great. The cooking process is not difficult, so even inexperienced chefs will find these recipes simple. You'll find a timetable for every type of food that you can prepare with your current model of Ninja Air Fryer and eat well while saving money on energy bills. Don't forget to ask your kids to test out the desserts!

So grab the ingredients, fire up your Ninja Air Fryer and revive your meal prep routine with unique recipes inspired by our love of food.

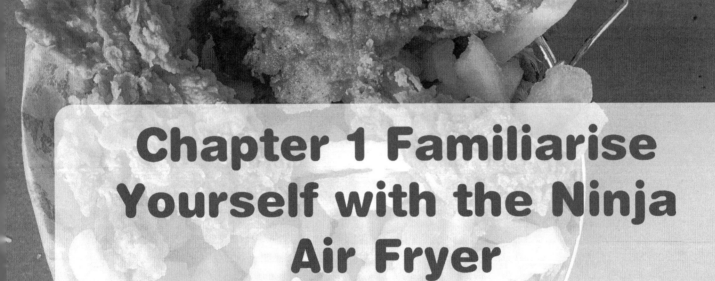

# Chapter 1 Familiarise Yourself with the Ninja Air Fryer

# Chapter 1 Familiarise Yourself with the Ninja Air Fryer

Ninja fans say that it's a must-have kitchen gadget for anyone who wants to cook food faster than conventional cooking methods, eat fat-free and healthily meals and save some pounds on energy bills. They say it right! You can literally cook delectable meals and sear meat to perfection just like those cooked over an open flame. Just put your basket of food in the air fryer, set a timer and wait for delicious results. And you don't have to worry about cleaning the mess after cooking because its removable parts make cleaning a breeze. Throw them away in the dishwasher and bring them out sparkling as new.

## How Does A Ninja Air Fryer Work?

The Ninja Air fryer cooks food by circulating hot air around the food evenly so that no part of it goes undercooked or overdone. This removes moisture from the food and creates a crunchy texture while keeping the ingredients moist from inside when frying and roasting the food. It has a capacity of 5.2L, a temperature control, 6 different cooking functions, and removable accessories for convenient cooking.

The Ninja Air Fryer makes cooking at home both fast and healthy by eliminating saturated fats found in traditional frying methods. No need for oil or any other type of fat when you're using an air fryer as it cooks food right in its own hot air chamber.

One 5.2-litre Air fryer can make meals to feed four to six people at one time. The cooking options are versatile—grill, bake, roast or air fry, dehydrate, or air crisp whatever you like and serve delicious portions around the dinner table faster than ever before. Just add ingredients and wait for them to cook. When it's time to eat, remove your food from the air fryer basket with tongs and place it on a plate. Serve yourself some french fries or chicken wings immediately—they'll be hot and crispy right away.

## Features for One-touch, Effortless Cooking

The Ninja Air Fryer is the perfect kitchen appliance for those who want to reduce the amount of fat in their diet without compromising on taste.

### Multiple Cooking Functions

The Ninja Air Fryer provides six different cooking functions that allow you to make tasty dishes using little or no oil. Instantly crisp your favourite frozen foods in a few minutes without defrosting using Max crisp. Airtight bake will keep food warm after it has come out of the oven, the air fry function will cook food with up to 75% less fat than traditional frying methods. You'll love the roast function that enables you to simmer ingredients at lower temperatures. Also, save time by pre-cooking your favourite foods using dehydrate functions and reheat the leftovers quickly on the go with roast function.

### Faster Cooking

The Ninja air fryer is the perfect solution for anyone who wants to cook a meal in less time and with less effort than other methods such as deep frying (which requires extra oil). In just 7 to 8 minutes, you'll have a portion of perfectly golden French fries that are crispy on the outside and tender inside—and not greasy at all!

### More Meal Choices

The Ninja Air Fryer lets you prepare a variety of dishes in large quantities, so everyone can enjoy them. You can use it to make tasty snacks, chicken wings, steaks, fish fillets and other seafood dishes.

### Energy Savings

The Ninja air fryer is a great way to cut down on energy usage and save money. It uses up to 55% less energy than a conventional oven, which can help you save hundreds of sterlings each year.

Cook Large Portions of Meals in One Go

One 5.2-litre Air fryer can make meals to feed six people at one time. Which means you can cook large portions of a meal in one setting and cut down on cooking time and energy usage. This is a great feature for big families or those who often arrange family gatherings.

## Cooking Tips for Fun and Easy Cooking

The Ninja air fryers use a streamlined cooking process that eliminates the dangers of using conventional ovens and stoves.

Here are some tips for getting the best results from your Ninja:

♦ It's very simple to use; power on, set the temp, set the time, and press start (Preheat for 3 mins too).

♦ For the best results, slice your favourite foods into small pieces and place them in the basket of your air fryer. It's important not to crowd your food or it will not cook evenly.

♦ If you want to add extra flavourings, spray or coat your food with oil and sprinkle some black pepper.

♦ To ensure even heating, we recommend using the crisper plate every time you air fry food. And to get your food extra crispy, shake or toss it with silicone-tipped tongs while cooking—every few minutes works best.

♦ Use parchment paper or another non-stick cooking surface when preparing foods such as chicken nuggets, fish fillets and vegetables. This will prevent sticking and make clean up easier if there are any spills during cooking.

♦ Adapt recipes for your oven by using the Roast or Bake function and reducing the temperature 10 degrees Celsius. Check food frequently to avoid overcooking. If you are cooking more food than a recipe calls for, increase the cook time. Check your dish frequently to avoid overcooking.

♦ It is important to pat fruits and vegetables dry before placing them in a dehydrator, as moisture will cause the food to spoil. You should dehydrate fruits and vegetables for 6–8 hours.

♦ To ensure that your beef or poultry dries sufficiently, it is important to trim off all fat before dehydrating. It will take 5–7 hours for the jerky to dehydrate. For more crispier results, you can extend the time.

## Cleaning and Care for Better Shelf Life

Cleaning your air fryer regularly will help you get more years of use out of it. Our must-have cleaning tips will show you how to clean your air fryer without any hassle, so that—when the time comes for another feast!—you'll be ready.

♦ The basket is easy to wash by hand and in a dishwasher (but it would be bulky in it). Wash removable parts by hand with warm, soapy water or spray them with a good degreasing dish detergent/oven cleaner mixture. Let stand for 10 minutes before washing off the solution and dry thoroughly.

♦ It has a non-stick coating that makes it easy to clean without any scrubbing or soaking required. The drip tray has small holes so when you cook food, any excess juice drains into these trays instead of onto your countertop (which prevents grease from causing stains).

♦ Clean the interior of your appliance with a damp cloth and use a gentle all-purpose cleaner or non abrasive scrubber to clean any areas where oil/grease has built up. Dry the appliance with a lint-free towel.

♦ Store your air fryer with the basket removed to allow for airflow and prevent moisture buildup —which is bad news for your fried foods!

# Chapter 2 Snacks and Appetisers

# Chapter 2 Snacks and Appetisers

## Crispy Tex-Mex Tortilla Chips

**Prep time: 5 minutes | Cook time: 5 minutes | Serves 4**

| | |
|---|---|
| Olive oil | ½ teaspoon paprika |
| ½ teaspoon salt | Pinch cayenne pepper |
| ½ teaspoon ground cumin | 8 (6-inch) corn tortillas, each |
| ½ teaspoon chilli powder | cut into 6 wedges |

1. Spray fryer basket lightly with olive oil. 2. In a small bowl, combine the salt, cumin, chilli powder, paprika, and cayenne pepper. 3. Place the tortilla wedges in the air fryer basket in a single layer. Spray the tortillas lightly with oil and sprinkle with some of the seasoning mixture. You will need to cook the tortillas in batches. 4. Air fry at 190ºC for 2 to 3 minutes. Shake the basket and cook until the chips are light brown and crispy, an additional 2 to 3 minutes. Watch the chips closely so they do not burn.

## Cabbage Pot Stickers

**Prep time: 12 minutes | Cook time: 11 to 18 minutes | Makes 12 pot stickers**

| | |
|---|---|
| 240 ml shredded red cabbage | 2 garlic cloves, minced |
| 60 ml chopped button mushrooms | 2 teaspoons grated fresh ginger |
| 60 ml grated carrot | 12 gyoza/pot sticker wrappers |
| 2 tablespoons minced onion | 2½ teaspoons olive oil, divided |

1. In a baking pan, combine the red cabbage, mushrooms, carrot, onion, garlic, and ginger. Add 1 tablespoon of water. Place in the air fryer and air fry at 190ºC for 3 to 6 minutes, until the vegetables are crisp-tender. Drain and set aside. 2. Working one at a time, place the pot sticker wrappers on a work surface. Top each wrapper with a scant 1 tablespoon of the filling. Fold half of the wrapper over the other half to form a half circle. Dab one edge with water and press both edges together. 3. To another pan, add 1¼ teaspoons of olive oil. Put half of the pot stickers, seam-side up, in the pan. Air fry for 5 minutes, or until the bottoms are light golden brown. Add 1 tablespoon of water and return the pan to the air fryer. 4. Air fry for 4 to 6 minutes more, or until hot. Repeat with the remaining pot stickers, remaining 1¼ teaspoons of oil, and another tablespoon of water. Serve immediately.

## Spicy Chickpeas

**Prep time: 5 minutes | Cook time: 17 minutes | Serves 3**

| | |
|---|---|
| Oil, for spraying | ½ teaspoon ground cumin |
| 1 (439 g) can chickpeas, drained | ½ teaspoon salt |
| | ½ teaspoon granulated garlic |
| 1 teaspoon chilli powder | 2 teaspoons lime juice |

1. Line the air fryer basket with parchment and spray lightly with oil. Place the chickpeas in the prepared basket. 2. Air fry at 200ºC for 17 minutes, shaking or stirring the chickpeas and spraying lightly with oil every 5 to 7 minutes. 3. In a small bowl, mix together the chilli powder, cumin, salt, and garlic. 4. When 2 to 3 minutes of cooking time remain, sprinkle half of the seasoning mix over the chickpeas. Finish cooking. 5. Transfer the chickpeas to a medium bowl and toss with the remaining seasoning mix and the lime juice. Serve immediately.

## Poutine with Waffle Fries

**Prep time: 10 minutes | Cook time: 15 to 17 minutes | Serves 4**

| | |
|---|---|
| 475 ml frozen waffle cut fries | 2 spring onions, sliced |
| 2 teaspoons olive oil | 240 ml shredded Swiss cheese |
| 1 red pepper, chopped | 120 ml bottled chicken gravy |

1. Preheat the air fryer to 190ºC. 2. Toss the waffle fries with the olive oil and place in the air fryer basket. Air fry for 10 to 12 minutes, or until the fries are crisp and light golden brown, shaking the basket halfway through the cooking time. 3. Transfer the fries to a baking pan and top with the pepper, spring onions, and cheese. Air fry for 3 minutes, or until the vegetables are crisp and tender. 4. Remove the pan from the air fryer and drizzle the gravy over the fries. Air fry for 2 minutes, or until the gravy is hot. 5. Serve immediately.

## Roasted Mushrooms with Garlic

**Prep time: 3 minutes | Cook time: 22 to 27 minutes | Serves 4**

16 garlic cloves, peeled

2 teaspoons olive oil, divided

16 button mushrooms

½ teaspoon dried marjoram

⅛ teaspoon freshly ground black pepper

1 tablespoon white wine or low-salt vegetable broth

1. In a baking pan, mix the garlic with 1 teaspoon of olive oil. Roast in the air fryer at 175ºC for 12 minutes. 2. Add the mushrooms, marjoram, and pepper. Stir to coat. Drizzle with the remaining 1 teaspoon of olive oil and the white wine. 3. Return to the air fryer and roast for 10 to 15 minutes more, or until the mushrooms and garlic cloves are tender. Serve.

## Five-Ingredient Falafel with Garlic-Yoghurt Sauce

**Prep time: 5 minutes | Cook time: 15 minutes | Serves 4**

Falafel:

1 (425 g) can chickpeas, drained and rinsed

120 ml fresh parsley

2 garlic cloves, minced

½ tablespoon ground cumin

1 tablespoon wholemeal flour

Salt

Garlic-Yoghurt Sauce:

240 ml non-fat plain Greek yoghurt

1 garlic clove, minced

1 tablespoon chopped fresh dill

2 tablespoons lemon juice

Make the Falafel: 1. Preheat the air fryer to 180ºC. 2. Put the chickpeas into a food processor. Pulse until mostly chopped, then add the parsley, garlic, and cumin and pulse for another 1 to 2 minutes, or until the ingredients are combined and turning into a dough. 3. Add the flour. Pulse a few more times until combined. The dough will have texture, but the chickpeas should be pulsed into small bits. 4. Using clean hands, roll the dough into 8 balls of equal size, then pat the balls down a bit so they are about ½-thick disks. 5. Spray the basket of the air fryer with olive oil cooking spray, then place the falafel patties in the basket in a single layer, making sure they don't touch each other. 6. Fry in the air fryer for 15 minutes. Make the garlic-yoghurt sauce 7. In a small bowl, combine the yoghurt, garlic, dill, and lemon juice. 8. Once the falafel is done cooking and nicely browned on all sides, remove them from the air fryer and season with salt. 9. Serve hot with a side of dipping sauce.

## Yummy Hush Puppies

**Prep time: 45 minutes | Cook time: 10 minutes | Serves 12**

240 ml self-raising yellow cornmeal

120 ml plain flour

1 teaspoon sugar

1 teaspoon salt

1 teaspoon freshly ground black pepper

1 large egg

80 ml canned creamed corn

240 ml minced onion

2 teaspoons minced jalapeño pepper

2 tablespoons olive oil, divided

1. Thoroughly combine the cornmeal, flour, sugar, salt, and pepper in a large bowl. 2. Whisk together the egg and corn in a small bowl. Pour the egg mixture into the bowl of cornmeal mixture and stir to combine. Stir in the minced onion and jalapeño. Cover the bowl with plastic wrap and place in the refrigerator for 30 minutes. 3. Preheat the air fryer to 190ºC. Line the air fryer basket with parchment paper and lightly brush it with 1 tablespoon of olive oil. 4. Scoop out the cornmeal mixture and form into 24 balls, about 1 inch. 5. Arrange the balls in the parchment paper-lined basket, leaving space between each ball. 6. Air fry in batches for 5 minutes. Shake the basket and brush the balls with the remaining 1 tablespoon of olive oil. Continue cooking for 5 minutes until golden brown. 7. Remove the balls (hush puppies) from the basket and serve on a plate.

## Sweet Bacon Potato Crunchies

**Prep time: 5 minutes | Cook time: 7 minutes | Serves 4**

24 frozen potato crunchies

6 slices cooked bacon

2 tablespoons maple syrup

240 ml shredded Cheddar cheese

1. Preheat the air fryer to 200ºC. 2. Put the potato crunchies in the air fryer basket. Air fry for 10 minutes, shaking the basket halfway through the cooking time. 3. Meanwhile, cut the bacon into 1-inch pieces. 4. Remove the potato crunchies from the air fryer basket and put into a baking pan. Top with the bacon and drizzle with the maple syrup. Air fry for 5 minutes, or until the crunchies and bacon are crisp. 5. Top with the cheese and air fry for 2 minutes, or until the cheese is melted. 6. Serve hot.

## Bacon-Wrapped Pickle Spears

**Prep time: 10 minutes | Cook time: 8 minutes | Serves 4**

| | |
|---|---|
| 8 to 12 slices bacon | cheese |
| 60 ml soft white cheese | 8 dill pickle spears |
| 60 ml shredded Mozzarella | 120 ml ranch dressing |

1. Lay the bacon slices on a flat surface. In a medium bowl, combine the soft white cheese and Mozzarella. Stir until well blended. Spread the cheese mixture over the bacon slices. 2. Place a pickle spear on a bacon slice and roll the bacon around the pickle in a spiral, ensuring the pickle is fully covered. (You may need to use more than one slice of bacon per pickle to fully cover the spear.) Tuck in the ends to ensure the bacon stays put. Repeat to wrap all the pickles. 3. Place the wrapped pickles in the air fryer basket in a single layer. Set the air fryer to 200ºC for 8 minutes, or until the bacon is cooked through and crisp on the edges. 4. Serve the pickle spears with ranch dressing on the side.

## Chilli-Brined Fried Calamari

**Prep time: 20 minutes | Cook time: 8 minutes | Serves 2**

| | |
|---|---|
| 1 (227 g) jar sweet or hot pickled cherry peppers | black pepper, to taste |
| 227 g calamari bodies and tentacles, bodies cut into ½-inch-wide rings | 3 large eggs, lightly beaten |
| | Cooking spray |
| | 120 ml mayonnaise |
| 1 lemon | 1 teaspoon finely chopped |
| 475 ml plain flour | rosemary |
| Rock salt and freshly ground | 1 garlic clove, minced |

1. Drain the pickled pepper brine into a large bowl and tear the peppers into bite-size strips. Add the pepper strips and calamari to the brine and let stand in the refrigerator for 20 minutes or up to 2 hours. 2. Grate the lemon zest into a large bowl then whisk in the flour and season with salt and pepper. Dip the calamari and pepper strips in the egg, then toss them in the flour mixture until fully coated. Spray the calamari and peppers liberally with cooking spray, then transfer half to the air fryer. Air fry at 200ºC, shaking the basket halfway into cooking, until the calamari is cooked through and golden brown, about 8 minutes. Transfer to a plate and repeat with the remaining pieces. 3. In a small bowl, whisk together the mayonnaise, rosemary, and garlic. Squeeze half the zested lemon to get 1 tablespoon of juice and stir it into the sauce. Season with salt and pepper. Cut the remaining zested lemon half into 4 small wedges and serve alongside the calamari, peppers, and sauce.

## Crunchy Pickle Chips

**Prep time: 30 minutes | Cook time: 12 minutes | Serves 4**

| | |
|---|---|
| Oil, for spraying | 475 ml plain flour |
| 475 ml sliced dill or sweet pickles, drained | 2 large eggs, beaten |
| | 475 ml panko breadcrumbs |
| 240 ml buttermilk | ¼ teaspoon salt |

1. Line the air fryer basket with parchment and spray lightly with oil. 2. In a shallow bowl, combine the pickles and buttermilk and let soak for at least 1 hour, then drain. 3. Place the flour, beaten eggs, and breadcrumbs in separate bowls. 4. Coat each pickle chip lightly in the flour, dip in the eggs, and dredge in the breadcrumbs. Be sure each one is evenly coated. 5. Place the pickle chips in the prepared basket, sprinkle with the salt, and spray lightly with oil. You may need to work in batches, depending on the size of your air fryer. 6. Air fry at 200ºC for 5 minutes, flip, and cook for another 5 to 7 minutes, or until crispy. Serve hot.

## Crispy Green Bean Fries with Lemon-Yoghurt Sauce

**Prep time: 5 minutes | Cook time: 5 minutes | Serves 4**

| | |
|---|---|
| Green Beans: | 227 g whole green beans |
| 1 egg | Lemon-Yoghurt Sauce: |
| 2 tablespoons water | 120 ml non-fat plain Greek |
| 1 tablespoon wholemeal flour | yoghurt |
| ¼ teaspoon paprika | 1 tablespoon lemon juice |
| ½ teaspoon garlic powder | ¼ teaspoon salt |
| ½ teaspoon salt | ⅛ teaspoon cayenne pepper |
| 60 ml wholemeal breadcrumbs | |

Make the Green Beans: 1. Preheat the air fryer to 190ºC. 2. In a medium shallow bowl, beat together the egg and water until frothy. 3. In a separate medium shallow bowl, whisk together the flour, paprika, garlic powder, and salt, then mix in the breadcrumbs. 4. Spray the bottom of the air fryer with cooking spray. 5. Dip each green bean into the egg mixture, then into the bread crumb mixture, coating the outside with the crumbs. Place the green beans in a single layer in the bottom of the air fryer basket. 6. Fry in the air fryer for 5 minutes, or until the breading is golden brown. Make the Lemon-Yoghurt Sauce: 7. In a small bowl, combine the yoghurt, lemon juice, salt, and cayenne. 8. Serve the green bean fries alongside the lemon-yoghurt sauce as a snack or appetizer.

## Spicy Tortilla Chips

**Prep time: 5 minutes | Cook time: 8 to 12 minutes | Serves 4**

½ teaspoon ground cumin
½ teaspoon paprika
½ teaspoon chilli powder
½ teaspoon salt

Pinch cayenne pepper
8 (6-inch) corn tortillas, each cut into 6 wedges
Cooking spray

1. Preheat the air fryer to 190ºC. Lightly spritz the air fryer basket with cooking spray. 2. Stir together the cumin, paprika, chilli powder, salt, and pepper in a small bowl. 3. Working in batches, arrange the tortilla wedges in the air fryer basket in a single layer. Lightly mist them with cooking spray. Sprinkle some seasoning mixture on top of the tortilla wedges. 4. Air fry for 4 to 6 minutes, shaking the basket halfway through, or until the chips are lightly browned and crunchy. 5. Repeat with the remaining tortilla wedges and seasoning mixture. 6. Let the tortilla chips cool for 5 minutes and serve.

## Garlicky and Cheesy French Fries

**Prep time: 5 minutes | Cook time: 20 to 25 minutes | Serves 4**

3 medium russet or Maris Piper potatoes, rinsed, dried, and cut into thin wedges or classic fry shapes
2 tablespoons extra-virgin olive oil
1 tablespoon granulated garlic

80 ml grated Parmesan cheese
½ teaspoon salt
¼ teaspoon freshly ground black pepper
Cooking oil spray
2 tablespoons finely chopped fresh parsley (optional)

1. In a large bowl combine the potato wedges or fries and the olive oil. Toss to coat. 2. Sprinkle the potatoes with the granulated garlic, Parmesan cheese, salt, and pepper, and toss again. 3. Insert the crisper plate into the basket and the basket into the unit. Preheat the unit by selecting AIR FRY, setting the temperature to 200ºC, and setting the time to 3 minutes. Select START/STOP to begin. 4. Once the unit is preheated, spray the crisper plate with cooking oil. Place the potatoes into the basket. 5. Select AIR FRY, set the temperature to 200ºC, and set the time to 20 to 25 minutes. Select START/STOP to begin. 6. After about 10 minutes, remove the basket and shake it so the fries at the bottom come up to the top. Reinsert the basket to resume cooking. 7. When the cooking is complete, top the fries with the parsley (if using) and serve hot.

## Garlic-Parmesan Croutons

**Prep time: 3 minutes | Cook time: 12 minutes | Serves 4**

Oil, for spraying
1 L cubed French bread
1 tablespoon grated Parmesan cheese

3 tablespoons olive oil
1 tablespoon granulated garlic
½ teaspoon unsalted salt

1. Line the air fryer basket with parchment and spray lightly with oil. 2. In a large bowl, mix together the bread, Parmesan cheese, olive oil, garlic, and salt, tossing with your hands to evenly distribute the seasonings. Transfer the coated bread cubes to the prepared basket. 3. Air fry at 175ºC for 10 to 12 minutes, stirring once after 5 minutes, or until crisp and golden brown.

## Artichoke and Olive Pitta Flatbread

**Prep time: 5 minutes | Cook time: 10 minutes | Serves 4**

2 wholewheat pittas
2 tablespoons olive oil, divided
2 garlic cloves, minced
¼ teaspoon salt
120 ml canned artichoke hearts, sliced

60 ml Kalamata olives
60 ml shredded Parmesan
60 ml crumbled feta
Chopped fresh parsley, for garnish (optional)

1. Preheat the air fryer to 190ºC. 2. Brush each pitta with 1 tablespoon olive oil, then sprinkle the minced garlic and salt over the top. 3. Distribute the artichoke hearts, olives, and cheeses evenly between the two pittas, and place both into the air fryer to bake for 10 minutes. 4. Remove the pittas and cut them into 4 pieces each before serving. Sprinkle parsley over the top, if desired.

## Air Fried Popcorn with Garlic Salt

**Prep time: 3 minutes | Cook time: 10 minutes | Serves 2**

2 tablespoons olive oil
60 ml popcorn kernels

1 teaspoon garlic salt

1. Preheat the air fryer to 190ºC. 2. Tear a square of aluminium foil the size of the bottom of the air fryer and place into the air fryer. 3. Drizzle olive oil over the top of the foil, and then pour in the popcorn kernels. 4. Roast for 8 to 10 minutes, or until the popcorn stops popping. 5. Transfer the popcorn to a large bowl and sprinkle with garlic salt before serving.

## Veggie Shrimp Toast

### Prep time: 15 minutes | Cook time: 3 to 6 minutes | Serves 4

8 large raw shrimp, peeled and finely chopped

1 egg white

2 garlic cloves, minced

3 tablespoons minced red pepper

1 medium celery stalk, minced

2 tablespoons cornflour

¼ teaspoon Chinese five-spice powder

3 slices firm thin-sliced no-salt wholemeal bread

1. Preheat the air fryer to 175°C. 2. In a small bowl, stir together the shrimp, egg white, garlic, red pepper, celery, cornflour, and five-spice powder. Top each slice of bread with one-third of the shrimp mixture, spreading it evenly to the edges. With a sharp knife, cut each slice of bread into 4 strips. 3. Place the shrimp toasts in the air fryer basket in a single layer. You may need to cook them in batches. Air fry for 3 to 6 minutes, until crisp and golden brown. 4. Serve hot.

## Air Fried Pot Stickers

### Prep time: 10 minutes | Cook time: 18 to 20 minutes | Makes 30 pot stickers

120 ml finely chopped cabbage

60 ml finely chopped red pepper

2 spring onions, finely chopped

1 egg, beaten

2 tablespoons cocktail sauce

2 teaspoons low-salt soy sauce

30 wonton wrappers

1 tablespoon water, for brushing the wrappers

1. Preheat the air fryer to 180°C. 2. In a small bowl, combine the cabbage, pepper, spring onions, egg, cocktail sauce, and soy sauce, and mix well. 3. Put about 1 teaspoon of the mixture in the centre of each wonton wrapper. Fold the wrapper in half, covering the filling; dampen the edges with water, and seal. You can crimp the edges of the wrapper with your fingers, so they look like the pot stickers you get in restaurants. Brush them with water. 4. Place the pot stickers in the air fryer basket and air fry in 2 batches for 9 to 10 minutes, or until the pot stickers are hot and the bottoms are lightly browned. 5. Serve hot.

## Tangy Fried Pickle Spears

### Prep time: 5 minutes | Cook time: 15 minutes | Serves 6

2 jars sweet and sour pickle spears, patted dry

2 medium-sized eggs

80 ml milk

1 teaspoon garlic powder

1 teaspoon sea salt

½ teaspoon shallot powder

⅓ teaspoon chilli powder

80 ml plain flour

Cooking spray

1. Preheat the air fryer to 195°C. Spritz the air fryer basket with cooking spray. 2. In a bowl, beat together the eggs with milk. In another bowl, combine garlic powder, sea salt, shallot powder, chilli powder and plain flour until well blended. 3. One by one, roll the pickle spears in the powder mixture, then dredge them in the egg mixture. Dip them in the powder mixture a second time for additional coating. 4. Arrange the coated pickles in the prepared basket. Air fry for 15 minutes until golden and crispy, shaking the basket halfway through to ensure even cooking. 5. Transfer to a plate and let cool for 5 minutes before serving.

# Chapter 3 Vegetables and Sides

# Chapter 3 Vegetables and Sides

## Spiced Butternut Squash

**Prep time: 10 minutes | Cook time: 15 minutes | Serves 4**

600 g 1-inch-cubed butternut squash

2 tablespoons vegetable oil

1 to 2 tablespoons brown sugar

1 teaspoon Chinese five-spice powder

1. In a medium bowl, combine the squash, oil, sugar, and five-spice powder. Toss to coat. 2. Place the squash in the air fryer basket. Set the air fryer to 200ºC for 15 minutes or until tender.

## Chiles Rellenos with Red Chile Sauce

**Prep time: 20 minutes | Cook time: 20 minutes | Serves 2**

Peppers:

2 poblano peppers, rinsed and dried

110 g thawed frozen or drained canned corn kernels

1 spring onion, sliced

2 tablespoons chopped fresh coriander

½ teaspoon coarse sea salt

¼ teaspoon black pepper

150 g grated Monterey Jack cheese

Sauce:

3 tablespoons extra-virgin olive

oil

25 g finely chopped yellow onion

2 teaspoons minced garlic

1 (170 g) can tomato paste

2 tablespoons ancho chili powder

1 teaspoon dried oregano

1 teaspoon ground cumin

½ teaspoon coarse sea salt

470 ml chicken stock

2 tablespoons fresh lemon juice

Mexican crema or sour cream, for serving

1. For the peppers: Place the peppers in the air fryer basket. Set the air fryer to 200ºC for 10 minutes, turning the peppers halfway through the cooking time, until their skins are charred. Transfer the peppers to a resealable plastic bag, seal, and set aside to steam for 5 minutes. Peel the peppers and discard the skins. Cut a slit down the centre of each pepper, starting at the stem and continuing to the tip. Remove the seeds, being careful not to tear the chile. 2. In a medium bowl, combine the corn, spring onion, coriander, salt, black pepper, and cheese; set aside. 3. Meanwhile, for the sauce: In a large skillet, heat the olive oil over medium-high heat. Add the onion and cook, stirring, until tender, about 5 minutes. Add the garlic and cook, stirring, for 30 seconds. Stir in the tomato paste, chile powder, oregano, and cumin, and salt. Cook, stirring, for 1 minute. Whisk in the stock and lemon juice. Bring to a simmer and cook, stirring occasionally, while the stuffed peppers finish cooking. 4. Cut a slit down the centre of each poblano pepper, starting at the stem and continuing to the tip. Remove the seeds, being careful not to tear the chile. 5. Carefully stuff each pepper with half the corn mixture. Place the stuffed peppers in a baking pan. Place the pan in the air fryer basket. Set the air fryer to 200ºC for 10 minutes, or until the cheese has melted. 6. Transfer the stuffed peppers to a serving platter and drizzle with the sauce and some crema.

## Sesame Taj Tofu

**Prep time: 5 minutes | Cook time: 25 minutes | Serves 4**

1 block firm tofu, pressed and cut into 1-inch thick cubes

2 tablespoons soy sauce

2 teaspoons toasted sesame

seeds

1 teaspoon rice vinegar

1 tablespoon cornflour

1. Preheat the air fryer to 200ºC. 2. Add the tofu, soy sauce, sesame seeds, and rice vinegar in a bowl together and mix well to coat the tofu cubes. Then cover the tofu in cornflour and put it in the air fryer basket. 3. Air fry for 25 minutes, giving the basket a shake at five-minute intervals to ensure the tofu cooks evenly. 4. Serve immediately.

## Easy Rosemary Green Beans

Prep time: 5 minutes | Cook time: 5 minutes | Serves 1

1 tablespoon butter, melted

2 tablespoons rosemary

½ teaspoon salt

3 cloves garlic, minced

95 g chopped green beans

1. Preheat the air fryer to 200ºC. 2. Combine the melted butter with the rosemary, salt, and minced garlic. Toss in the green beans, coating them well. 3. Air fry for 5 minutes. 4. Serve immediately.

## Caramelized Aubergine with Harissa Yogurt

**Prep time: 10 minutes | Cook time: 15 minutes | Serves 2**

| | |
|---|---|
| 1 medium aubergine (about 340 g), cut crosswise into ½-inch-thick slices and quartered | ground black pepper, to taste |
| | 120 g plain yogurt (not Greek) |
| 2 tablespoons vegetable oil | 2 tablespoons harissa paste |
| coarse sea salt and freshly | 1 garlic clove, grated |
| | 2 teaspoons honey |

1. In a bowl, toss together the aubergine and oil, season with salt and pepper, and toss to coat evenly. Transfer to the air fryer and air fry at 200ºC, shaking the basket every 5 minutes, until the aubergine is caramelized and tender, about 15 minutes. 2. Meanwhile, in a small bowl, whisk together the yogurt, harissa, and garlic, then spread onto a serving plate. 3. Pile the warm aubergine over the yogurt and drizzle with the honey just before serving.

## Fried Curried Fruit

**Prep time: 10 minutes | Cook time: 20 minutes | Serves 6 to 8**

| | |
|---|---|
| 210 g cubed fresh pineapple | 425 g can dark, sweet, pitted cherries with juice |
| 200 g cubed fresh pear (firm, not overly ripe) | |
| | 2 tablespoons brown sugar |
| 230 g frozen peaches, thawed | 1 teaspoon curry powder |

1. Combine all ingredients in large bowl. Stir gently to mix in the sugar and curry. 2. Pour into a baking pan and bake at 180ºC for 10 minutes. 3. Stir fruit and cook 10 more minutes. 4. Serve hot.

## Parmesan-Rosemary Radishes

**Prep time: 5 minutes | Cook time: 15 to 20 minutes | Serves 4**

| | |
|---|---|
| 1 bunch radishes, stemmed, trimmed, and quartered | 1 tablespoon chopped fresh rosemary |
| 1 tablespoon avocado oil | Sea salt and freshly ground black pepper, to taste |
| 2 tablespoons finely grated fresh Parmesan cheese | |

1. Place the radishes in a medium bowl and toss them with the avocado oil, Parmesan cheese, rosemary, salt, and pepper. 2. Set the air fryer to190ºC. Arrange the radishes in a single layer in the air fryer basket. Roast for 15 to 20 minutes, until golden brown and tender. Let cool for 5 minutes before serving.

## Cheesy Dinner Rolls

**Prep time: 10 minutes | Cook time: 12 minutes | Serves 6**

| | |
|---|---|
| 225 g shredded Mozzarella cheese | almond flour |
| | 40 g ground flaxseed |
| 30 g full-fat cream cheese | ½ teaspoon baking powder |
| 95 g blanched finely ground | 1 large egg |

1. Place Mozzarella, cream cheese, and almond flour in a large microwave-safe bowl. Microwave for 1 minute. Mix until smooth. 2. Add flaxseed, baking powder, and egg until fully combined and smooth. Microwave an additional 15 seconds if it becomes too firm. 3. Separate the dough into six pieces and roll into balls. Place the balls into the air fryer basket. 4. Adjust the temperature to 160ºC and air fry for 12 minutes. 5. Allow rolls to cool completely before serving.

## Fried Asparagus Spears

**Prep time: 5 minutes | Cook time: 12 minutes | Serves 4**

| | |
|---|---|
| 1 tablespoon olive oil | ¼ teaspoon ground black pepper |
| 450 g asparagus spears, ends trimmed | |
| | 1 tablespoon salted butter, melted |
| ¼ teaspoon salt | |

1. In a large bowl, drizzle olive oil over asparagus spears and sprinkle with salt and pepper. 2. Place spears into ungreased air fryer basket. Adjust the temperature to 190ºC and set the timer for 12 minutes, shaking the basket halfway through cooking. Asparagus will be lightly browned and tender when done. 3. Transfer to a large dish and drizzle with butter. Serve warm.

## Golden Garlicky Mushrooms

**Prep time: 10 minutes | Cook time: 10 minutes | Serves 4**

| | |
|---|---|
| 6 small mushrooms | 1 teaspoon parsley |
| 1 tablespoon bread crumbs | 1 teaspoon garlic purée |
| 1 tablespoon olive oil | Salt and ground black pepper, to taste |
| 30 g onion, peeled and diced | |

1. Preheat the air fryer to 180ºC. 2. Combine the bread crumbs, oil, onion, parsley, salt, pepper and garlic in a bowl. Cut out the mushrooms' stalks and stuff each cap with the crumb mixture. 3. Air fry in the air fryer for 10 minutes. 4. Serve hot.

## Ricotta Potatoes

**Prep time: 15 minutes | Cook time: 15 minutes | Serves 4**

| | |
|---|---|
| 4 potatoes | fresh parsley |
| 2 tablespoons olive oil | 1 tablespoon minced coriander |
| 110 g Ricotta cheese, at room temperature | 60 g Cheddar cheese, preferably freshly grated |
| 2 tablespoons chopped spring onions | 1 teaspoon celery seeds |
| | ½ teaspoon salt |
| 1 tablespoon roughly chopped | ½ teaspoon garlic pepper |

1. Preheat the air fryer to 180ºC. 2. Pierce the skin of the potatoes with a knife. 3. Air fry in the air fryer basket for 13 minutes. If they are not cooked through by this time, leave for 2 to 3 minutes longer. 4. In the meantime, make the stuffing by combining all the other ingredients. 5. Cut halfway into the cooked potatoes to open them. 6. Spoon equal amounts of the stuffing into each potato and serve hot.

## Super Cheesy Gold Aubergine

**Prep time: 15 minutes | Cook time: 30 minutes | Serves 4**

| | |
|---|---|
| 1 medium aubergine, peeled and cut into ½-inch-thick rounds | cheese |
| | Freshly ground black pepper, to taste |
| 1 teaspoon salt, plus more for seasoning | Cooking oil spray |
| 60 g plain flour | 180 g marinara sauce |
| 2 eggs | 45 g shredded Parmesan cheese, divided |
| 90 g Italian bread crumbs | 110 g shredded Mozzarella cheese, divided |
| 2 tablespoons grated Parmesan | |

1. Blot the aubergine with paper towels to dry completely. You can also sprinkle with 1 teaspoon of salt to sweat out the moisture; if you do this, rinse the aubergine slices and blot dry again. 2. Place the flour in a shallow bowl. 3. In another shallow bowl, beat the eggs. 4. In a third shallow bowl, stir together the bread crumbs and grated Parmesan cheese and season with salt and pepper. 5. Dip each aubergine round in the flour, in the eggs, and into the bread crumbs to coat. 6. Insert the crisper plate into the basket and the basket into the unit. Preheat the unit by selecting AIR FRY, setting the temperature to 200ºC, and setting the time to 3 minutes. Select START/STOP to begin. 7. Once the unit is preheated, spray the crisper plate and the basket with cooking oil. Working in batches, place the aubergine rounds into the basket. Do not stack them. Spray the aubergine with the cooking oil. 8. Select AIR FRY, set the temperature to 200ºC, and set the time to 10 minutes. Select START/STOP to begin. 9. After 7 minutes, open the unit and top each round with 1 teaspoon of marinara sauce and ½ tablespoon each of shredded Parmesan and Mozzarella cheese. Resume cooking for 2 to 3 minutes until the cheese melts. 10. Repeat steps 5, 6, 7, 8, and 9 with the remaining aubergine. 11. When the cooking is complete, serve immediately.

## Curry Roasted Cauliflower

**Prep time: 10 minutes | Cook time: 20 minutes | Serves 4**

| | |
|---|---|
| 65 ml olive oil | 1 head cauliflower, cut into bite-size florets |
| 2 teaspoons curry powder | |
| ½ teaspoon salt | ½ red onion, sliced |
| ¼ teaspoon freshly ground black pepper | 2 tablespoons freshly chopped parsley, for garnish (optional) |

1. Preheat the air fryer to 200ºC. 2. In a large bowl, combine the olive oil, curry powder, salt, and pepper. Add the cauliflower and onion. Toss gently until the vegetables are completely coated with the oil mixture. Transfer the vegetables to the basket of the air fryer. 3. Pausing about halfway through the cooking time to shake the basket, air fry for 20 minutes until the cauliflower is tender and beginning to brown. Top with the parsley, if desired, before serving.

## Fried Courgette Salad

**Prep time: 10 minutes | Cook time: 5 to 7 minutes | Serves 4**

| | |
|---|---|
| 2 medium courgette, thinly sliced | Zest and juice of ½ lemon |
| 5 tablespoons olive oil, divided | 1 clove garlic, minced |
| 15 g chopped fresh parsley | 65 g crumbled feta cheese |
| 2 tablespoons chopped fresh mint | Freshly ground black pepper, to taste |

1. Preheat the air fryer to 200ºC. 2. In a large bowl, toss the courgette slices with 1 tablespoon of the olive oil. 3. Working in batches if necessary, arrange the courgette slices in an even layer in the air fryer basket. Pausing halfway through the cooking time to shake the basket, air fry for 5 to 7 minutes until soft and lightly browned on each side. 4. Meanwhile, in a small bowl, combine the remaining 4 tablespoons olive oil, parsley, mint, lemon zest, lemon juice, and garlic. 5. Arrange the courgette on a plate and drizzle with the dressing. Sprinkle the feta and black pepper on top. Serve warm or at room temperature.

## Cheesy Flatbread

**Prep time: 5 minutes | Cook time: 7 minutes | Serves 2**

| | |
|---|---|
| 225 g shredded Mozzarella cheese | almond flour |
| 25 g blanched finely ground | 30 g full-fat cream cheese, softened |

1. In a large microwave-safe bowl, melt Mozzarella in the microwave for 30 seconds. Stir in almond flour until smooth and then add cream cheese. Continue mixing until dough forms, gently kneading it with wet hands if necessary. 2. Divide the dough into two pieces and roll out to ¼-inch thickness between two pieces of parchment. Cut another piece of parchment to fit your air fryer basket. 3. Place a piece of flatbread onto your parchment and into the air fryer, working in two batches if needed. 4. Adjust the temperature to 160ºC and air fry for 7 minutes. 5. Halfway through the cooking time flip the flatbread. Serve warm.

## Glazed Sweet Potato Bites

**Prep time: 10 minutes | Cook time: 25 minutes | Serves 4**

| | |
|---|---|
| Oil, for spraying | 2 tablespoons honey |
| 3 medium sweet potatoes, peeled and cut into 1-inch pieces | 1 tablespoon olive oil |
| | 2 teaspoons ground cinnamon |

1. Line the air fryer basket with parchment and spray lightly with oil. 2. In a large bowl, toss together the sweet potatoes, honey, olive oil, and cinnamon until evenly coated. 3. Place the potatoes in the prepared basket. 4. Air fry at 200ºC for 20 to 25 minutes, or until crispy and easily pierced with a fork.

## Spicy Roasted Bok Choy

**Prep time: 10 minutes | Cook time: 7 to 10 minutes | Serves 4**

| | |
|---|---|
| 2 tablespoons olive oil | 2 cloves garlic, minced |
| 2 tablespoons reduced-sodium coconut aminos | 1 head (about 450 g) bok choy, sliced lengthwise into quarters |
| 2 teaspoons sesame oil | 2 teaspoons black sesame seeds |
| 2 teaspoons chili-garlic sauce | |

1. Preheat the air fryer to 200ºC. 2. In a large bowl, combine the olive oil, coconut aminos, sesame oil, chili-garlic sauce, and garlic. Add the bok choy and toss, massaging the leaves with your hands if necessary, until thoroughly coated. 3. Arrange the bok choy in the basket of the air fryer. Pausing about halfway through the cooking time to shake the basket, air fry for 7 to 10 minutes until the bok choy is tender and the tips of the leaves begin to crisp. 4.Remove from the basket and let cool for a few minutes before coarsely chopping. Serve sprinkled with the sesame seeds.

## Glazed Carrots

**Prep time: 10 minutes | Cook time: 8 to 10 minutes | Serves 4**

| | |
|---|---|
| 2 teaspoons honey | 450 g baby carrots |
| 1 teaspoon orange juice | 2 teaspoons olive oil |
| ½ teaspoon grated orange rind | ¼ teaspoon salt |
| ⅛ teaspoon ginger | |

1. Combine honey, orange juice, grated rind, and ginger in a small bowl and set aside. 2. Toss the carrots, oil, and salt together to coat well and pour them into the air fryer basket. 3. Roast at 200ºC for 5 minutes. Shake basket to stir a little and cook for 2 to 4 minutes more, until carrots are barely tender. 4. Pour carrots into a baking pan. 5. Stir the honey mixture to combine well, pour glaze over carrots, and stir to coat. 6. Roast at 180ºC for 1 minute or just until heated through.

## Baked Jalapeño and Cheese Cauliflower Mash

**Prep time: 10 minutes | Cook time: 15 minutes | Serves 6**

| | |
|---|---|
| 1 (340 g) steamer bag cauliflower florets, cooked according to package instructions | 120 g shredded sharp Cheddar cheese |
| 2 tablespoons salted butter, softened | 20 g pickled jalapeños |
| | ½ teaspoon salt |
| 60 g cream cheese, softened | ¼ teaspoon ground black pepper |

1. Place cooked cauliflower into a food processor with remaining ingredients. Pulse twenty times until cauliflower is smooth and all ingredients are combined. 2. Spoon mash into an ungreased round nonstick baking dish. Place dish into air fryer basket. Adjust the temperature to 190ºC and bake for 15 minutes. The top will be golden brown when done. Serve warm.

# Hawaiian Brown Rice

**Prep time: 10 minutes | Cook time: 12 to 16 minutes | Serves 4 to 6**

| | |
|---|---|
| 110 g ground sausage | 380 g cooked brown rice |
| 1 teaspoon butter | 1 (230 g) can crushed |
| 20 g minced onion | pineapple, drained |
| 40 g minced bell pepper | |

1. Shape sausage into 3 or 4 thin patties. Air fry at 200ºC for 6 to 8 minutes or until well done. Remove from air fryer, drain, and crumble. Set aside. 2. Place butter, onion, and bell pepper in baking pan. Roast at 200ºC for 1 minute and stir. Cook 3 to 4 minutes longer or just until vegetables are tender. 3. Add sausage, rice, and pineapple to vegetables and stir together. 4. Roast for 2 to 3 minutes, until heated through.

# Crispy Turnip Fries

**Prep time: 10 minutes | Cook time: 20 to 30 minutes | Serves 4**

| | |
|---|---|
| 900 g turnip, peeled and cut into ¼ to ½-inch fries | Salt and freshly ground black pepper, to taste |
| 2 tablespoons olive oil | |

1. Preheat the air fryer to 200ºC. 2. In a large bowl, combine the turnip and olive oil. Season to taste with salt and black pepper. Toss gently until thoroughly coated. 3. Working in batches if necessary, spread the turnip in a single layer in the air fryer basket. Pausing halfway through the cooking time to shake the basket, air fry for 20 to 30 minutes until the fries are lightly browned and crunchy.

# Cheese Courgette Fritters

**Prep time: 10 minutes | Cook time: 10 minutes | Serves 4**

| | |
|---|---|
| 2 courgette, grated (about 450 g) | ¼ teaspoon dried thyme |
| 1 teaspoon salt | ¼ teaspoon ground turmeric |
| 25 g almond flour | ¼ teaspoon freshly ground |
| 20 g grated Parmesan cheese | black pepper |
| 1 large egg | 1 tablespoon olive oil |
| | ½ lemon, sliced into wedges |

1. Preheat the air fryer to 200ºC. Cut a piece of parchment paper to fit slightly smaller than the bottom of the air fryer. 2. Place the courgette in a large colander and sprinkle with the salt. Let sit for 5 to 10 minutes. Squeeze as much liquid as you can from the courgette and place in a large mixing bowl. Add the almond flour, Parmesan, egg, thyme, turmeric, and black pepper. Stir gently until thoroughly combined. 3. Shape the mixture into 8 patties and arrange on the parchment paper. Brush lightly with the olive oil. Pausing halfway through the cooking time to turn the patties, air fry for 10 minutes until golden brown. Serve warm with the lemon wedges.

# Roasted Radishes with Sea Salt

**Prep time: 5 minutes | Cook time: 18 minutes | Serves 4**

| | |
|---|---|
| 450 g radishes, ends trimmed if needed | 2 tablespoons olive oil |
| | ½ teaspoon sea salt |

1. Preheat the air fryer to 180ºC. 2. In a large bowl, combine the radishes with olive oil and sea salt. 3. Pour the radishes into the air fryer and roast for 10 minutes. Stir or turn the radishes over and roast for 8 minutes more, then serve.

# Cauliflower Steaks Gratin

**Prep time: 10 minutes | Cook time: 13 minutes | Serves 2**

| | |
|---|---|
| 1 head cauliflower | thyme leaves |
| 1 tablespoon olive oil | 3 tablespoons grated |
| Salt and freshly ground black pepper, to taste | Parmigiano-Reggiano cheese |
| ½ teaspoon chopped fresh | 2 tablespoons panko bread crumbs |

1. Preheat the air fryer to 190ºC. 2. Cut two steaks out of the centre of the cauliflower. To do this, cut the cauliflower in half and then cut one slice about 1-inch thick off each half. The rest of the cauliflower will fall apart into florets, which you can roast on their own or save for another meal. 3. Brush both sides of the cauliflower steaks with olive oil and season with salt, freshly ground black pepper and fresh thyme. Place the cauliflower steaks into the air fryer basket and air fry for 6 minutes. Turn the steaks over and air fry for another 4 minutes. Combine the Parmesan cheese and panko bread crumbs and sprinkle the mixture over the tops of both steaks and air fry for another 3 minutes until the cheese has melted and the bread crumbs have browned. Serve this with some sautéed bitter greens and air-fried blistered tomatoes.

## Blistered Shishito Peppers with Lime Juice

### Prep time: 5 minutes | Cook time: 9 minutes | Serves 3

| | |
|---|---|
| 230 g shishito peppers, rinsed | 1 tablespoon tamari or shoyu |
| Cooking spray | 2 teaspoons fresh lime juice |
| Sauce: | 2 large garlic cloves, minced |

1. Preheat the air fryer to 200°C. Spritz the air fryer basket with cooking spray. 2. Place the shishito peppers in the basket and spritz them with cooking spray. Roast for 3 minutes. 3. Meanwhile, whisk together all the ingredients for the sauce in a large bowl. Set aside. 4. Shake the basket and spritz them with cooking spray again, then roast for an additional 3 minutes. 5. Shake the basket one more time and spray the peppers with cooking spray. Continue roasting for 3 minutes until the peppers are blistered and nicely browned. 6. Remove the peppers from the basket to the bowl of sauce. Toss to coat well and serve immediately.

## Sweet and Crispy Roasted Pearl Onions

### Prep time: 5 minutes | Cook time: 18 minutes | Serves 3

| | |
|---|---|
| 1 (410 g) package frozen pearl onions (do not thaw) | 2 teaspoons finely chopped fresh rosemary |
| 2 tablespoons extra-virgin olive oil | ½ teaspoon coarse sea salt |
| 2 tablespoons balsamic vinegar | ¼ teaspoon black pepper |

1. In a medium bowl, combine the onions, olive oil, vinegar, rosemary, salt, and pepper until well coated. 2. Transfer the onions to the air fryer basket. Set the air fryer to 200°C for 18 minutes, or until the onions are tender and lightly charred, stirring once or twice during the cooking time.

## Indian Aubergine Bharta

### Prep time: 15 minutes | Cook time: 20 minutes | Serves 4

| | |
|---|---|
| 1 medium aubergine | 2 tablespoons fresh lemon juice |
| 2 tablespoons vegetable oil | 2 tablespoons chopped fresh coriander |
| 25 g finely minced onion | |
| 100 g finely chopped fresh tomato | ½ teaspoon coarse sea salt |
| | ⅛ teaspoon cayenne pepper |

1. Rub the aubergine all over with the vegetable oil. Place the aubergine in the air fryer basket. Set the air fryer to 200°C for 20 minutes, or until the aubergine skin is blistered and charred. 2. Transfer the aubergine to a re-sealable plastic bag, seal, and set aside for 15 to 20 minutes (the aubergine will finish cooking in the residual heat trapped in the bag). 3. Transfer the aubergine to a large bowl. Peel off and discard the charred skin. Roughly mash the aubergine flesh. Add the onion, tomato, lemon juice, coriander, salt, and cayenne. Stir to combine.

## Panko Broccoli Tots

### Prep time: 15 minutes | Cook time: 10 minutes | Makes 24 tots

| | |
|---|---|
| 230 g broccoli florets | 2 tablespoons grated Parmesan cheese |
| 1 egg, beaten | |
| ⅛ teaspoon onion powder | 25 g panko bread crumbs |
| ¼ teaspoon salt | Oil for misting |
| ⅛ teaspoon pepper | |

1. Steam broccoli for 2 minutes. Rinse in cold water, drain well, and chop finely. 2. In a large bowl, mix broccoli with all other ingredients except the oil. 3. Scoop out small portions of mixture and shape into 24 tots. Lay them on a cookie sheet or wax paper as you work. 4. Spray tots with oil and place in air fryer basket in single layer. 5. Air fry at 200°C for 5 minutes. Shake basket and spray with oil again. Cook 5 minutes longer or until browned and crispy.

## Sausage-Stuffed Mushroom Caps

### Prep time: 10 minutes | Cook time: 8 minutes | Serves 2

| | |
|---|---|
| 6 large portobello mushroom caps | 2 tablespoons blanched finely ground almond flour |
| 230 g Italian sausage | 20 g grated Parmesan cheese |
| 15 g chopped onion | 1 teaspoon minced fresh garlic |

1. Use a spoon to hollow out each mushroom cap, reserving scrapings. 2. In a medium skillet over medium heat, brown the sausage about 10 minutes or until fully cooked and no pink remains. Drain and then add reserved mushroom scrapings, onion, almond flour, Parmesan, and garlic. Gently fold ingredients together and continue cooking an additional minute, then remove from heat. 3. Evenly spoon the mixture into mushroom caps and place the caps into a 6-inch round pan. Place pan into the air fryer basket. 4. Adjust the temperature to 190°C and set the timer for 8 minutes. 5. When finished cooking, the tops will be browned and bubbling. Serve warm.

# Garlicky Tofu Bites

**Prep time: 15 minutes | Cook time: 30 minutes | Serves 4**

1 packaged firm tofu, cubed and pressed to remove excess water

1 tablespoon soy sauce

1 tablespoon ketchup

1 tablespoon maple syrup

½ teaspoon vinegar

1 teaspoon liquid smoke

1 teaspoon hot sauce

2 tablespoons sesame seeds

1 teaspoon garlic powder

Salt and ground black pepper, to taste

Cooking spray

1. Preheat the air fryer to 190°C. 2. Spritz a baking dish with cooking spray. 3. Combine all the ingredients to coat the tofu completely and allow the marinade to absorb for half an hour. 4. Transfer the tofu to the baking dish, then air fry for 15 minutes. Flip the tofu over and air fry for another 15 minutes on the other side. 5. Serve immediately.

# Chapter 4 Fish and Seafood

# Chapter 4 Fish and Seafood

## Crab Cakes with Bell Peppers

**Prep time: 5 minutes | Cook time: 10 minutes | Serves 4**

| | |
|---|---|
| 230 g jumbo lump crab meat | 35 g diced red bell pepper |
| 1 egg, beaten | 60 g mayonnaise |
| Juice of ½ lemon | 1 tablespoon Old Bay seasoning |
| 50 g bread crumbs | 1 teaspoon plain flour |
| 35 g diced green bell pepper | Cooking spray |

1. Preheat the air fryer to 190ºC. 2. Make the crab cakes: Place all the ingredients except the flour and oil in a large bowl and stir until well incorporated. 3. Divide the crab mixture into four equal portions and shape each portion into a patty with your hands. Top each patty with a sprinkle of ¼ teaspoon of flour. 4. Arrange the crab cakes in the air fryer basket and spritz them with cooking spray. 5. Air fry for 10 minutes, flipping the crab cakes halfway through, or until they are cooked through. 6. Divide the crab cakes among four plates and serve.

## Seasoned Breaded Prawns

**Prep time: 15 minutes | Cook time: 10 to 15 minutes | Serves 4**

| | |
|---|---|
| 2 teaspoons Old Bay seasoning, divided | deveined, with tails on |
| ½ teaspoon garlic powder | 2 large eggs |
| ½ teaspoon onion powder | 75 g whole-wheat panko bread crumbs |
| 455 g large prawns, peeled and | Cooking spray |

1. Preheat the air fryer to 190ºC. 2. Spray the air fryer basket lightly with cooking spray. 3. In a medium bowl, mix together 1 teaspoon of Old Bay seasoning, garlic powder, and onion powder. Add the prawns and toss with the seasoning mix to lightly coat. 4. In a separate small bowl, whisk the eggs with 1 teaspoon water. 5. In a shallow bowl, mix together the remaining 1 teaspoon Old Bay seasoning and the panko bread crumbs. 6. Dip each prawns in the egg mixture and dredge in the bread crumb mixture to evenly coat. 7. Place the prawns in the air fryer basket, in a single layer. Lightly spray the prawns with cooking spray. You many need to cook the prawns in batches. 8. Air fry for 10 to 15 minutes, or until the prawns is cooked through and crispy, shaking the basket at 5-minute intervals to redistribute and evenly cook. 9. Serve immediately.

## Garlic Lemon Scallops

**Prep time: 5 minutes | Cook time: 10 minutes | Serves 4**

| | |
|---|---|
| 4 tablespoons salted butter, melted | 8 sea scallops, 30 g each, cleaned and patted dry |
| 4 teaspoons peeled and finely minced garlic | ¼ teaspoon salt |
| ½ small lemon, zested and juiced | ¼ teaspoon ground black pepper |

1. In a small bowl, mix butter, garlic, lemon zest, and lemon juice. Place scallops in an ungreased round nonstick baking dish. Pour butter mixture over scallops, then sprinkle with salt and pepper. 2. Place dish into air fryer basket. Adjust the temperature to 180ºC and bake for 10 minutes. Scallops will be opaque and firm, and have an internal temperature of 55ºC when done. Serve warm.

## Chilean Sea Bass with Olive Relish

**Prep time: 10 minutes | Cook time: 10 minutes | Serves 2**

| | |
|---|---|
| Olive oil spray | ½ teaspoon kosher or coarse sea salt |
| 2 (170 g) Chilean sea bass fillets or other firm-fleshed white fish | ½ teaspoon black pepper |
| 3 tablespoons extra-virgin olive oil | 60 g pitted green olives, diced |
| ½ teaspoon ground cumin | 10 g finely diced onion |
| | 1 teaspoon chopped capers |

1. Spray the air fryer basket with the olive oil spray. Drizzle the fillets with the olive oil and sprinkle with the cumin, salt, and pepper. Place the fish in the air fryer basket. Set the air fryer to 165ºC for 10 minutes, or until the fish flakes easily with a fork. 2. Meanwhile, in a small bowl, stir together the olives, onion, and capers. 3. Serve the fish topped with the relish.

## Thai Prawn Skewers with Peanut Dipping Sauce

**Prep time: 15 minutes | Cook time: 6 minutes | Serves 2**

Salt and pepper, to taste

340 g extra-large prawns, peeled and deveined

1 tablespoon vegetable oil

1 teaspoon honey

½ teaspoon grated lime zest plus 1 tablespoon juice, plus lime wedges for serving

6 (6-inch) wooden skewers

3 tablespoons creamy peanut butter

3 tablespoons hot tap water

1 tablespoon chopped fresh coriander

1 teaspoon fish sauce

1. Preheat the air fryer to 200ºC. 2. Dissolve 2 tablespoons salt in 1 litre cold water in a large container. Add prawns, cover, and refrigerate for 15 minutes. 3. Remove prawns from brine and pat dry with paper towels. Whisk oil, honey, lime zest, and ¼ teaspoon pepper together in a large bowl. Add prawns and toss to coat. Thread prawns onto skewers, leaving about ¼ inch between each prawns (3 or 4 prawns per skewer). 4. Arrange 3 skewers in air fryer basket, parallel to each other and spaced evenly apart. Arrange remaining 3 skewers on top, perpendicular to the bottom layer. Air fry until prawns are opaque throughout, 6 to 8 minutes, flipping and rotating skewers halfway through cooking. 5. Whisk peanut butter, hot tap water, lime juice, coriander, and fish sauce together in a bowl until smooth. Serve skewers with peanut dipping sauce and lime wedges.

## BBQ Prawns with Creole Butter Sauce

**Prep time: 10 minutes | Cook time: 12 to 15 minutes | Serves 4**

6 tablespoons unsalted butter

80 ml Worcestershire sauce

3 cloves garlic, minced

Juice of 1 lemon

1 teaspoon paprika

1 teaspoon Creole seasoning

680 g large uncooked prawns, peeled and deveined

2 tablespoons fresh parsley

1. Preheat the air fryer to 190ºC. 2. In a large microwave-safe bowl, combine the butter, Worcestershire, and garlic. Microwave on high for 1 to 2 minutes until the butter is melted. Stir in the lemon juice, paprika, and Creole seasoning. Add the prawns and toss until thoroughly coated. 3. Transfer the mixture to a casserole dish or pan that fits in your air fryer. Pausing halfway through the cooking time to turn the prawns, air fry for 12 to 15 minutes, until the prawns are cooked through. Top with the parsley just before serving.

## Scallops in Lemon-Butter Sauce

**Prep time: 10 minutes | Cook time: 6 minutes | Serves 2**

8 large dry sea scallops (about 340 g)

Salt and freshly ground black pepper, to taste

2 tablespoons olive oil

2 tablespoons unsalted butter, melted

2 tablespoons chopped flat-leaf parsley

1 tablespoon fresh lemon juice

2 teaspoons capers, drained and chopped

1 teaspoon grated lemon zest

1 clove garlic, minced

1. Preheat the air fryer to 200ºC. 2. Use a paper towel to pat the scallops dry. Sprinkle lightly with salt and pepper. Brush with the olive oil. Arrange the scallops in a single layer in the air fryer basket. Pausing halfway through the cooking time to turn the scallops, air fry for about 6 minutes until firm and opaque. 3. Meanwhile, in a small bowl, combine the oil, butter, parsley, lemon juice, capers, lemon zest, and garlic. Drizzle over the scallops just before serving.

## Crustless Prawn Quiche

**Prep time: 15 minutes | Cook time: 20 minutes | Serves 2**

Vegetable oil

4 large eggs

120 ml single cream

110 g raw prawns, chopped

120 g shredded Parmesan or Swiss cheese

235 g chopped spring onions

1 teaspoon sweet smoked paprika

1 teaspoon Herbes de Provence

1 teaspoon black pepper

½ to 1 teaspoon kosher or coarse sea salt

1. Generously grease a baking pan with vegetable oil. (Be sure to grease the pan well, the proteins in eggs stick something fierce. Alternatively, line the bottom of the pan with baking paper cut to fit and spray the baking paper and sides of the pan generously with vegetable oil spray.) 2. In a large bowl, beat together the eggs and single cream. Add the prawns, 90 g of the cheese, the scallions, paprika, Herbes de Provence, pepper, and salt. Stir with a fork to thoroughly combine. Pour the egg mixture into the prepared pan. 3. Place the pan in the air fryer basket. Set the air fryer to 150ºC for 20 minutes. After 17 minutes, sprinkle the remaining 30 g cheese on top and cook for the remaining 3 minutes, or until the cheese has melted, the eggs are set, and a toothpick inserted into the center comes out clean. 4. Serve the quiche warm or at room temperature.

## Parmesan-Crusted Halibut Fillets

**Prep time: 5 minutes | Cook time: 10 minutes | Serves 4**

| | |
|---|---|
| 2 medium-sized halibut fillets | and freshly cracked mixed |
| Dash of tabasco sauce | peppercorns, to taste |
| 1 teaspoon curry powder | 2 eggs |
| ½ teaspoon ground coriander | 1½ tablespoons olive oil |
| ½ teaspoon hot paprika | 75 g grated Parmesan cheese |
| Kosher or coarse sea salt, | |

1. Preheat the air fryer to 185°C. 2. On a clean work surface, drizzle the halibut fillets with the tabasco sauce. Sprinkle with the curry powder, coriander, hot paprika, salt, and cracked mixed peppercorns. Set aside. 3. In a shallow bowl, beat the eggs until frothy. In another shallow bowl, combine the olive oil and Parmesan cheese. 4. One at a time, dredge the halibut fillets in the beaten eggs, shaking off any excess, then roll them over the Parmesan cheese until evenly coated. 5. Arrange the halibut fillets in the air fryer basket in a single layer and air fry for 10 minutes, or until the fish is golden brown and crisp. 6. Cool for 5 minutes before serving.

## Asian Marinated Salmon

**Prep time: 30 minutes | Cook time: 6 minutes | Serves 2**

| | |
|---|---|
| Marinade: | 1¼ inches thick) |
| 60 ml wheat-free tamari or coconut aminos | Sliced spring onions, for garnish |
| 2 tablespoons lime or lemon juice | Sauce (Optional): |
| 2 tablespoons sesame oil | 60 ml beef stock |
| 2 tablespoons powdered sweetener | 60 ml wheat-free tamari |
| 2 teaspoons grated fresh ginger | 3 tablespoons powdered sweetener |
| 2 cloves garlic, minced | 1 tablespoon tomato sauce |
| ½ teaspoon ground black pepper | ⅛ teaspoon guar gum or xanthan gum (optional, for thickening) |
| 2 (110 g) salmon fillets (about | |

1. Make the marinade: In a medium-sized shallow dish, stir together all the ingredients for the marinade until well combined. Place the salmon in the marinade. Cover and refrigerate for at least 2 hours or overnight. 2. Preheat the air fryer to 200°C. 3. Remove the salmon fillets from the marinade and place them in the air fryer, leaving space between them. Air fry for 6 minutes, or until the salmon is cooked through and flakes easily with a fork. 4. While the salmon cooks, make the sauce, if using: Place all the sauce ingredients except the guar gum in a medium-sized bowl and stir until well combined. Taste and adjust the sweetness to your liking. While whisking slowly, add the guar gum. Allow the sauce to thicken for 3 to 5 minutes. (The sauce can be made up to 3 days ahead and stored in an airtight container in the fridge.) Drizzle the sauce over the salmon before serving. 5. Garnish the salmon with sliced spring onions before serving. Store leftovers in an airtight container in the fridge for up to 3 days. Reheat in a preheated 175°C air fryer for 3 minutes, or until heated through.

## Mediterranean-Style Cod

**Prep time: 5 minutes | Cook time: 12 minutes | Serves 4**

| | |
|---|---|
| 4 cod fillets, 170 g each | 6 cherry tomatoes, halved |
| 3 tablespoons fresh lemon juice | 45 g pitted and sliced kalamata olives |
| 1 tablespoon olive oil | olives |
| ¼ teaspoon salt | |

1. Place cod into an ungreased round nonstick baking dish. Pour lemon juice into dish and drizzle cod with olive oil. Sprinkle with salt. Place tomatoes and olives around baking dish in between fillets. 2. Place dish into air fryer basket. Adjust the temperature to 175°C and bake for 12 minutes, carefully turning cod halfway through cooking. Fillets will be lightly browned, easily flake, and have an internal temperature of at least 65°C when done. Serve warm.

## Sea Bass with Roasted Root Vegetables

**Prep time: 10 minutes | Cook time: 15 minutes | Serves 4**

| | |
|---|---|
| 1 carrot, diced small | 4 sea bass fillets |
| 1 parsnip, diced small | ½ teaspoon onion powder |
| 1 swede, diced small | 2 garlic cloves, minced |
| 60 ml olive oil | 1 lemon, sliced, plus additional |
| 1 teaspoon salt, divided | wedges for serving |

1. Preheat the air fryer to 190°C. 2. In a small bowl, toss the carrot, parsnip, and swede with olive oil and 1 teaspoon salt. 3. Lightly season the sea bass with the remaining 1 teaspoon of salt and the onion powder, then place it into the air fryer basket in a single layer. 4. Spread the garlic over the top of each fillet, then cover with lemon slices. 5. Pour the prepared vegetables into the basket around and on top of the fish. Roast for 15 minutes. 6. Serve with additional lemon wedges if desired.

## Homemade Chilli Prawns

**Prep time: 10 minutes | Cook time: 8 minutes | Serves 2**

| | |
|---|---|
| 8 prawns, peeled and deveined | ½ teaspoon garlic powder |
| Salt and black pepper, to taste | ½ teaspoon ground cumin |
| ½ teaspoon ground cayenne pepper | ½ teaspoon red chilli flakes |
| | Cooking spray |

1. Preheat the air fryer to 170ºC. Spritz the air fryer basket with cooking spray. 2. Toss the remaining ingredients in a large bowl until the prawns are well coated. 3. Spread the coated prawns evenly in the basket and spray them with cooking spray. 4. Air fry for 8 minutes, flipping the prawns halfway through, or until the prawns are pink. 5. Remove the prawns from the basket to a plate.

## Roasted Cod with Lemon-Garlic Potatoes

**Prep time: 10 minutes | Cook time: 28 minutes | Serves 2**

| | |
|---|---|
| 3 tablespoons unsalted butter, softened, divided | 340 g), unpeeled, sliced ¼ inch thick |
| 2 garlic cloves, minced | 1 tablespoon minced fresh parsley, chives, or tarragon |
| 1 lemon, grated to yield 2 teaspoons zest and sliced ¼ inch thick | 2 (230 g) skinless cod fillets, 1¼ inches thick |
| Salt and pepper, to taste | Vegetable oil spray |
| 1 large russet potato (about | |

1. Preheat the air fryer to 200ºC. 2. Make foil sling for air fryer basket by folding 1 long sheet of aluminum foil so it is 4 inches wide. Lay sheet of foil widthwise across basket, pressing foil into and up sides of basket. Fold excess foil as needed so that edges of foil are flush with top of basket. Lightly spray the foil and basket with vegetable oil spray. 3. Microwave 1 tablespoon butter, garlic, 1 teaspoon lemon zest, ¼ teaspoon salt, and ⅛ teaspoon pepper in a medium bowl, stirring once, until the butter is melted and the mixture is fragrant, about 30 seconds. Add the potato slices and toss to coat. Shingle the potato slices on sling in prepared basket to create 2 even layers. Air fry until potato slices are spotty brown and just tender, 16 to 18 minutes, using a sling to rotate potatoes halfway through cooking. 4. Combine the remaining 2 tablespoons butter, remaining 1 teaspoon lemon zest, and parsley in a small bowl. Pat the cod dry with paper towels and season with salt and pepper. Place the fillets, skinned-side down, on top of potato slices, spaced evenly apart. (Tuck thinner tail ends of fillets under themselves as needed to create uniform pieces.) Dot the fillets with the butter mixture and top with the lemon slices. Return the basket to the air fryer and air fry until the cod flakes apart when gently prodded with a paring knife and registers 60ºC, 12 to 15 minutes, using a sling to rotate the potato slices and cod halfway through cooking. 5. Using a sling, carefully remove potatoes and cod from air fryer. Cut the potato slices into 2 portions between fillets using fish spatula. Slide spatula along underside of potato slices and transfer with cod to individual plates. Serve.

## Easy Ahi Tuna Steaks

**Prep time: 5 minutes | Cook time: 14 minutes | Serves 2**

| | |
|---|---|
| 2 ahi tuna steaks, 170g each | 3 tablespoons everything bagel seasoning |
| 2 tablespoons olive oil | |

1. Drizzle both sides of each steak with olive oil. Place seasoning on a medium plate and press each side of tuna steaks into seasoning to form a thick layer. 2. Place steaks into ungreased air fryer basket. Adjust the temperature to200ºC and air fry for 14 minutes, turning steaks halfway through cooking. Steaks will be done when internal temperature is at least 65ºC for well-done. Serve warm.

## Baked Monkfish

**Prep time: 20 minutes | Cook time: 12 minutes | Serves 2**

| | |
|---|---|
| 2 teaspoons olive oil | or tamari |
| 100 g celery, sliced | 2 tablespoons lime juice |
| 2 bell peppers, sliced | Coarse salt and ground black pepper, to taste |
| 1 teaspoon dried thyme | |
| ½ teaspoon dried marjoram | 1 teaspoon cayenne pepper |
| ½ teaspoon dried rosemary | 90 g Kalamata olives, pitted and sliced |
| 2 monkfish fillets | |
| 1 tablespoon coconut aminos, | |

1. In a nonstick skillet, heat the olive oil for 1 minute. Once hot, sauté the celery and peppers until tender, about 4 minutes. Sprinkle with thyme, marjoram, and rosemary and set aside. 2. Toss the fish fillets with the coconut aminos, lime juice, salt, black pepper, and cayenne pepper. Place the fish fillets in the lightly greased air fryer basket and bake at 200ºC for 8 minutes. 3. Turn them over, add the olives, and cook an additional 4 minutes. Serve with the sautéed vegetables on the side. Bon appétit!

## Nutty Prawns with Amaretto Glaze

**Prep time: 30 minutes | Cook time: 10 minutes per batch | Serves 10 to 12**

| | |
|---|---|
| 120 g plain flour | oil |
| ½ teaspoon baking powder | 185 g sliced almonds |
| 1 teaspoon salt | 900 g large prawns (about |
| 2 eggs, beaten | 32 to 40 prawns), peeled and |
| 120 ml milk | deveined, tails left on |
| 2 tablespoons olive or vegetable | 470 ml amaretto liqueur |

1. Combine the flour, baking powder and salt in a large bowl. Add the eggs, milk and oil and stir until it forms a smooth batter. Coarsely crush the sliced almonds into a second shallow dish with your hands. 2. Dry the prawns well with paper towels. Dip the prawns into the batter and shake off any excess batter, leaving just enough to lightly coat the prawns. Transfer the prawns to the dish with the almonds and coat completely. Place the coated prawns on a plate or baking sheet and when all the prawns have been coated, freeze the prawns for an 1 hour, or as long as a week before air frying. 3. Preheat the air fryer to 200ºC. 4. Transfer 8 frozen prawns at a time to the air fryer basket. Air fry for 6 minutes. Turn the prawns over and air fry for an additional 4 minutes. Repeat with the remaining prawns. 5. While the prawns are cooking, bring the Amaretto to a boil in a small saucepan on the stovetop. Lower the heat and simmer until it has reduced and thickened into a glaze, about 10 minutes. 6. Remove the prawns from the air fryer and brush both sides with the warm amaretto glaze. Serve warm.

## Homemade Jalea

**Prep time: 20 minutes | Cook time: 10 minutes | Serves 4**

| | |
|---|---|
| Salsa Criolla☐ | fish if not using prawns) |
| ½ red onion, thinly sliced | 20 large or jumbo prawns, |
| 2 tomatoes, diced | peeled and deveined |
| 1 serrano or jalapeño pepper, | 30 g plain flour |
| deseeded and diced | 40 g cornflour |
| 1 clove garlic, minced | 1 teaspoon garlic powder |
| 5 g chopped fresh coriander | 1 teaspoon kosher or coarse sea |
| Pinch of kosher or coarse sea | salt |
| salt | ¼ teaspoon cayenne pepper |
| 3 limes | 240 g panko bread crumbs |
| Fried Seafood: | 2 eggs, beaten with 2 |
| 455 g firm, white-fleshed fish | tablespoons water |
| such as cod (add an extra 230 g | Vegetable oil, for spraying |

Mayonnaise or tartar sauce, for serving (optional)

1. To make the Salsa Criolla, combine the red onion, tomatoes, pepper, garlic, cilantro, and salt in a medium bowl. Add the juice and zest of 2 of the limes. Refrigerate the salad while you make the fish. 2. To make the seafood, cut the fish fillets into strips approximately 2 inches long and 1 inch wide. Place the flour, cornstarch, garlic powder, salt, and cayenne pepper on a plate and whisk to combine. Place the panko on a separate plate. Dredge the fish strips in the seasoned flour mixture, shaking off any excess. Dip the strips in the egg mixture, coating them completely, then dredge in the panko, shaking off any excess. Place the fish strips on a plate or rack. Repeat with the prawns, if using. 3. Spray the air fryer basket with oil, and preheat the air fryer to 200ºC. Working in 2 or 3 batches, arrange the fish and prawns in a single layer in the basket, taking care not to crowd the basket. Spray with oil. Air fry for 5 minutes, then flip and air fry for another 4 to 5 minutes until the outside is brown and crisp and the inside of the fish is opaque and flakes easily with a fork. Repeat with the remaining seafood. 4. Place the fried seafood on a platter. Use a slotted spoon to remove the salsa criolla from the bowl, leaving behind any liquid that has accumulated. Place the salsa criolla on top of the fried seafood. Serve immediately with the remaining lime, cut into wedges, and mayonnaise or tartar sauce as desired.

## Almond-Crusted Fish

**Prep time: 15 minutes | Cook time: 10 minutes | Serves 4**

| | |
|---|---|
| 4 firm white fish fillets, 110g | Salt and pepper, to taste |
| each | 940 g plain flour |
| 45 g breadcrumbs | 1 egg, beaten with 1 tablespoon |
| 20 g slivered almonds, crushed | water |
| 2 tablespoons lemon juice | Olive or vegetable oil for |
| ⅛ teaspoon cayenne | misting or cooking spray |

1. Split fish fillets lengthwise down the center to create 8 pieces. 2. Mix breadcrumbs and almonds together and set aside. 3. Mix the lemon juice and cayenne together. Brush on all sides of fish. 4. Season fish to taste with salt and pepper. 5. Place the flour on a sheet of wax paper. 6. Roll fillets in flour, dip in egg wash, and roll in the crumb mixture. 7. Mist both sides of fish with oil or cooking spray. 8. Spray the air fryer basket and lay fillets inside. 9. Roast at 200ºC for 5 minutes, turn fish over, and cook for an additional 5 minutes or until fish is done and flakes easily.

## Classic Fish Sticks with Tartar Sauce

**Prep time: 10 minutes | Cook time: 12 to 15 minutes | Serves 4**

| | |
|---|---|
| 680 g cod fillets, cut into 1-inch strips | 120 ml sour cream |
| 1 teaspoon salt | 120 ml mayonnaise |
| ½ teaspoon freshly ground black pepper | 3 tablespoons chopped dill pickle |
| 2 eggs | 2 tablespoons capers, drained and chopped |
| 70 g almond flour | ½ teaspoon dried dill |
| 20 g grated Parmesan cheese | 1 tablespoon dill pickle liquid (optional) |
| Tartar Sauce: | |

1. Preheat the air fryer to 200ºC. 2. Season the cod with the salt and black pepper; set aside. 3. In a shallow bowl, lightly beat the eggs. In a second shallow bowl, combine the almond flour and Parmesan cheese. Stir until thoroughly combined. 4. Working with a few pieces at a time, dip the fish into the egg mixture followed by the flour mixture. Press lightly to ensure an even coating. 5. Working in batches if necessary, arrange the fish in a single layer in the air fryer basket and spray lightly with olive oil. Pausing halfway through the cooking time to turn the fish, air fry for 12 to 15 minutes, until the fish flakes easily with a fork. Let sit in the basket for a few minutes before serving with the tartar sauce. 6. To make the tartar sauce: In a small bowl, combine the sour cream, mayonnaise, pickle, capers, and dill. If you prefer a thinner sauce, stir in the pickle liquid.

## Dukkah-Crusted Halibut

**Prep time: 15 minutes | Cook time: 17 minutes | Serves 2**

| | |
|---|---|
| Dukkah: | ¼ teaspoon black pepper |
| 1 tablespoon coriander seeds | Fish: |
| 1 tablespoon sesame seeds | 2 halibut fillets, 140 g each |
| 1½ teaspoons cumin seeds | 2 tablespoons mayonnaise |
| 50 g roasted mixed nuts | Vegetable oil spray |
| ¼ teaspoon kosher or coarse sea salt | Lemon wedges, for serving |

1. For the Dukkah: Combine the coriander, sesame seeds, and cumin in a small baking pan. Place the pan in the air fryer basket. Set the air fryer to 200ºC for 5 minutes. Toward the end of the cooking time, you will hear the seeds popping. Transfer to a plate and let cool for 5 minutes. 2. Transfer the toasted seeds to a food processor or spice grinder and add the mixed nuts. Pulse until coarsely chopped. Add the salt and pepper and stir well. 3. For

the fish: Spread each fillet with 1 tablespoon of the mayonnaise. Press a heaping tablespoon of the Dukkah into the mayonnaise on each fillet, pressing lightly to adhere. 4. Spray the air fryer basket with vegetable oil spray. Place the fish in the basket. Cook for 12 minutes, or until the fish flakes easily with a fork. 5. Serve the fish with lemon wedges.

## Honey-Glazed Salmon

**Prep time: 5 minutes | Cook time: 12 minutes | Serves 4**

| | |
|---|---|
| 60 ml raw honey | ½ teaspoon salt |
| 4 garlic cloves, minced | Olive oil cooking spray |
| 1 tablespoon olive oil | 4 (1½-inch-thick) salmon fillets |

1. Preheat the air fryer to 190ºC. 2. In a small bowl, mix together the honey, garlic, olive oil, and salt. 3. Spray the bottom of the air fryer basket with olive oil cooking spray, and place the salmon in a single layer on the bottom of the air fryer basket. 4. Brush the top of each fillet with the honey-garlic mixture, and roast for 10 to 12 minutes, or until the internal temperature reaches 65ºC.

## Fried Catfish Fillets

**Prep time: 10 minutes | Cook time: 20 minutes | Serves 4**

| | |
|---|---|
| 1 egg | ¼ teaspoon garlic powder |
| 100 g finely ground cornmeal | ¼ teaspoon freshly ground black pepper |
| 30 g plain flour | |
| ¾ teaspoon salt | 4 140 g catfish fillets, halved crosswise |
| 1 teaspoon paprika | |
| 1 teaspoon Old Bay seasoning | Olive oil spray |

1. In a shallow bowl, beat the egg with 2 tablespoons water. 2. On a plate, stir together the cornmeal, flour, salt, paprika, Old Bay, garlic powder, and pepper. 3. Dip the fish into the egg mixture and into the cornmeal mixture to coat. Press the cornmeal mixture into the fish and gently shake off any excess. 4. Insert the crisper plate into the basket and the basket into the unit to 200ºC. 5. Once the unit is preheated, place a baking paper liner into the basket. Place the coated fish on the liner and spray it with olive oil.. 6. Cook for 10 minutes, remove the basket and spray the fish with olive oil. Flip the fish and spray the other side with olive oil. Reinsert the basket to resume cooking. Check the fish after 7 minutes more. If the fish is golden and crispy and registers at least 65ºC on a food thermometer, it is ready. If not, resume cooking. 8. When the cooking is complete, serve.

## Cheesy Tuna Patties

**Prep time: 5 minutes | Cook time: 17 to 18 minutes | Serves 4**

Tuna Patties:
455 g canned tuna, drained
1 egg, whisked
2 tablespoons shallots, minced
1 garlic clove, minced
1 cup grated Romano cheese
Sea salt and ground black

pepper, to taste
1 tablespoon sesame oil
Cheese Sauce:
1 tablespoon butter
240 ml beer
2 tablespoons grated Cheddar
cheese

1. Mix together the canned tuna, whisked egg, shallots, garlic, cheese, salt, and pepper in a large bowl and stir to incorporate. 2. Divide the tuna mixture into four equal portions and form each portion into a patty with your hands. Refrigerate the patties for 2 hours. 3. When ready, brush both sides of each patty with sesame oil. 4. Preheat the air fryer to 180ºC. 5. Place the patties in the air fryer basket and bake for 14 minutes, flipping the patties halfway through, or until lightly browned and cooked through. 6. Meanwhile, melt the butter in a pan over medium heat. 7. Pour in the beer and whisk constantly, or until it begins to bubble. 8. Add the grated Colby cheese and mix well. Continue cooking for 3 to 4 minutes, or until the cheese melts. Remove the patties from the basket to a plate. Drizzle them with the cheese sauce and serve immediately.

## Prawn Dejonghe Skewers

**Prep time: 10 minutes | Cook time: 15 minutes | Serves 4**

2 teaspoons sherry, or apple
cider vinegar
3 tablespoons unsalted butter,
melted
120 g panko bread crumbs
3 cloves garlic, minced
8 g minced flat-leaf parsley,

plus more for garnish
1 teaspoon kosher salt
Pinch of cayenne pepper
680 g prawns, peeled and
deveined
Vegetable oil, for spraying
Lemon wedges, for serving

1. Stir the sherry and melted butter together in a shallow bowl or pie plate and whisk until combined. Set aside. Whisk together the panko, garlic, parsley, salt, and cayenne pepper on a large plate or shallow bowl. 2. Thread the prawns onto metal skewers designed for the air fryer or bamboo skewers, 3 to 4 per skewer. Dip 1 prawns skewer in the butter mixture, then dredge in the panko mixture until each prawns is lightly coated. Place the skewer on a plate or rimmed baking sheet and repeat the process with the remaining

skewers. 3. Preheat the air fryer to 175ºC. Arrange 4 skewers in the air fryer basket. Spray the skewers with oil and air fry for 8 minutes, until the bread crumbs are golden brown and the prawns are cooked through. Transfer the cooked skewers to a serving plate and keep warm while cooking the remaining 4 skewers in the air fryer. 4. Sprinkle the cooked skewers with additional fresh parsley and serve with lemon wedges if desired.

## Calamari with Hot Sauce

**Prep time: 10 minutes | Cook time: 6 minutes | Serves 2**

280 g calamari, trimmed
2 tablespoons hot sauce

1 tablespoon avocado oil

1. Slice the calamari and sprinkle with avocado oil. 2. Put the calamari in the air fryer and cook at 200ºC for 3 minutes per side. 3. Then transfer the calamari in the serving plate and sprinkle with hot sauce.

## Sea Bass with Avocado Cream

**Prep time: 30 minutes | Cook time: 9 minutes | Serves 4**

Fish Fillets:
1½ tablespoons balsamic
vinegar
120 ml vegetable broth
⅓ teaspoon shallot powder
1 tablespoon coconut aminos,
or tamari
4 Sea Bass fillets
1 teaspoon ground black pepper
1½ tablespoons olive oil
Fine sea salt, to taste
⅓ teaspoon garlic powder

Avocado Cream:
2 tablespoons Greek-style
yogurt
1 clove garlic, peeled and
minced
1 teaspoon ground black pepper
½ tablespoon olive oil
80 ml vegetable broth
1 avocado
½ teaspoon lime juice
⅓ teaspoon fine sea salt

1. In a bowl, wash and pat the fillets dry using some paper towels. Add all the seasonings. In another bowl, stir in the remaining ingredients for the fish fillets. 2. Add the seasoned fish fillets; cover and let the fillets marinate in your refrigerator at least 3 hours. 3. Then, set the air fryer to 165ºC. Cook marinated sea bass fillets in the air fryer grill basket for 9 minutes. 4. In the meantime, prepare the avocado sauce by mixing all the ingredients with an immersion blender or regular blender. Serve the sea bass fillets topped with the avocado sauce. Enjoy!

## Cucumber and Salmon Salad

**Prep time: 10 minutes | Cook time: 8 to 10 minutes | Serves 2**

455 g salmon fillet

1½ tablespoons olive oil, divided

1 tablespoon sherry vinegar

1 tablespoon capers, rinsed and drained

1 seedless cucumber, thinly

sliced

¼ white onion, thinly sliced

2 tablespoons chopped fresh parsley

Salt and freshly ground black pepper, to taste

1. Preheat the air fryer to 200°C. 2. Lightly coat the salmon with ½ tablespoon of the olive oil. Place skin-side down in the air fryer basket and air fry for 8 to 10 minutes until the fish is opaque and flakes easily with a fork. Transfer the salmon to a plate and let cool to room temperature. Remove the skin and carefully flake the fish into bite-size chunks. 3. In a small bowl, whisk the remaining 1 tablespoon olive oil and the vinegar until thoroughly combined. Add the flaked fish, capers, cucumber, onion, and parsley. Season to taste with salt and freshly ground black pepper. Toss gently to coat. Serve immediately or cover and refrigerate for up to 4 hours.

## Crab Cakes with Sriracha Mayonnaise

**Prep time: 15 minutes | Cook time: 10 minutes | Serves 4**

Sriracha Mayonnaise:

230 g mayonnaise

1 tablespoon Sriracha

1½ teaspoons freshly squeezed lemon juice

Crab Cakes:

1 teaspoon extra-virgin olive oil

40 g finely diced red bell pepper

40 g diced onion

40 g diced celery

455 g lump crab meat

1 teaspoon Old Bay seasoning

1 egg

1½ teaspoons freshly squeezed lemon juice

200 g panko bread crumbs, divided

Vegetable oil, for spraying

1. Mix the mayonnaise, Sriracha, and lemon juice in a small bowl. Place ⅔ of the mixture in a separate bowl to form the base of the crab cakes. Cover the remaining Sriracha mayonnaise and refrigerate. (This will become dipping sauce for the crab cakes once they are cooked.) 2. Heat the olive oil in a heavy-bottomed, medium skillet over medium-high heat. Add the bell pepper, onion, and celery and sauté for 3 minutes. Transfer the vegetables to the bowl with the reserved ⅔ of Sriracha mayonnaise. Mix in the crab, Old Bay seasoning, egg, and lemon juice. Add 120 g of the panko. Form the crab mixture into 8 cakes. Dredge the cakes in the remaining panko, turning to coat. Place on a baking sheet. Cover and refrigerate for at least 1 hour and up to 8 hours. 3. Preheat the air fryer to 190°C. Spray the air fryer basket with oil. Working in batches as needed so as not to overcrowd the basket, place the chilled crab cakes in a single layer in the basket. Spray the crab cakes with oil. Bake until golden brown, 8 to 10 minutes, carefully turning halfway through cooking. Remove to a platter and keep warm. Repeat with the remaining crab cakes as needed. Serve the crab cakes immediately with Sriracha mayonnaise dipping sauce.

## Pesto Prawns with Wild Rice Pilaf

**Prep time: 5 minutes | Cook time: 5 minutes | Serves 4**

455 g medium prawns, peeled and deveined

60 g pesto sauce

1 lemon, sliced

390 g cooked wild rice pilaf

1. Preheat the air fryer to 180°C. 2. In a medium bowl, toss the prawns with the pesto sauce until well coated. 3. Place the prawns in a single layer in the air fryer basket. Put the lemon slices over the prawns and roast for 5 minutes. 4. Remove the lemons and discard. Serve a quarter of the prawns over 100 g wild rice with some favorite steamed vegetables.

# Chapter 5 Poultry

# Chapter 5 Poultry

## Breaded Turkey Cutlets

**Prep time: 5 minutes | Cook time: 8 minutes | Serves 4**

60 g whole wheat bread crumbs

¼ teaspoon paprika

¼ teaspoon salt

¼ teaspoon black pepper

⅛ teaspoon dried sage

⅛ teaspoon garlic powder

1 egg

4 turkey breast cutlets

Chopped fresh parsley, for serving

1. Preheat the air fryer to 190ºC. 2. In a medium shallow bowl, whisk together the bread crumbs, paprika, salt, black pepper, sage, and garlic powder. 3. In a separate medium shallow bowl, whisk the egg until frothy. 4. Dip each turkey cutlet into the egg mixture, then into the bread crumb mixture, coating the outside with the crumbs. Place the breaded turkey cutlets in a single layer in the bottom of the air fryer basket, making sure that they don't touch each other. 5. Bake for 4 minutes. Turn the cutlets over, then bake for 4 minutes more, or until the internal temperature reaches 75ºC. Sprinkle on the parsley and serve.

## Pickle Brined Fried Chicken

**Prep time: 30 minutes | Cook time: 47 minutes | Serves 4**

4 bone-in, skin-on chicken legs, cut into drumsticks and thighs (about 1.6 kg)

Pickle juice from 1 (680 g) jar kosher dill pickles

60 g flour

Salt and freshly ground black pepper, to taste

2 eggs

120 g fine bread crumbs

1 teaspoon salt

1 teaspoon freshly ground black pepper

½ teaspoon ground paprika

⅛ teaspoon ground cayenne pepper

Vegetable or rapeseed oil

1. Place the chicken in a shallow dish and pour the pickle juice over the top. Cover and transfer the chicken to the refrigerator to brine in the pickle juice for 3 to 8 hours. 2. When you are ready to cook, remove the chicken from the refrigerator to let it come to room temperature while you set up a dredging station. Place the flour in a shallow dish and season well with salt and freshly ground black pepper. Whisk the eggs in a second shallow dish. In a third shallow dish, combine the bread crumbs, salt, pepper, paprika and cayenne pepper. 3. Preheat the air fryer to 190ºC. 4. Remove the chicken from the pickle brine and gently dry it with a clean kitchen towel. Dredge each piece of chicken in the flour, then dip it into the egg mixture, and finally press it into the bread crumb mixture to coat all sides of the chicken. Place the breaded chicken on a plate or baking sheet and spray each piece all over with vegetable oil. 5. Air fry the chicken in two batches. Place two chicken thighs and two drumsticks into the air fryer basket. Air fry for 10 minutes. Then, gently turn the chicken pieces over and air fry for another 10 minutes. Remove the chicken pieces and let them rest on plate, do not cover. Repeat with the second batch of chicken, air frying for 20 minutes, turning the chicken over halfway through. 6. Lower the temperature of the air fryer to 170ºC. Place the first batch of chicken on top of the second batch already in the basket and air fry for an additional 7 minutes. Serve warm and enjoy.

## Curried Orange Honey Chicken

**Prep time: 10 minutes | Cook time: 16 to 19 minutes | Serves 4**

340 g boneless, skinless chicken thighs, cut into 1-inch pieces

1 yellow bell pepper, cut into 1½-inch pieces

1 small red onion, sliced

Olive oil for misting

60 ml chicken stock

2 tablespoons honey

60 ml orange juice

1 tablespoon cornflour

2 to 3 teaspoons curry powder

1. Preheat the air fryer to 190ºC. 2. Put the chicken thighs, pepper, and red onion in the air fryer basket and mist with olive oil. 3. Roast for 12 to 14 minutes or until the chicken is cooked to 75ºC, shaking the basket halfway through cooking time. 4. Remove the chicken and vegetables from the air fryer basket and set aside. 5. In a metal bowl, combine the stock, honey, orange juice, cornflour, and curry powder, and mix well. Add the chicken and vegetables, stir, and put the bowl in the basket. 6. Return the basket to the air fryer and roast for 2 minutes. Remove and stir, then roast for 2 to 3 minutes or until the sauce is thickened and bubbly. 7. Serve warm.

## Easy Chicken Nachos

**Prep time: 5 minutes | Cook time: 5 minutes | Serves 8**

| | |
|---|---|
| Oil, for spraying | 55 g corn tortilla chips |
| 420 g shredded cooked chicken | 75 g bacon bits |
| 1 (30 g) package ranch seasoning | 235 g shredded Cheddar cheese |
| 60 g sour cream | 1 tablespoon chopped spring onions |

1. Line the air fryer basket with parchment and spray lightly with oil. 2. In a small bowl, mix together the chicken, ranch seasoning, and sour cream. 3. Place the tortilla chips in the prepared basket and top with the chicken mixture. Add the bacon bits, Cheddar cheese, and spring onions. 4. Air fry at 220ºC for 3 to 5 minutes, or until heated through and the cheese is melted.

## Chicken and Gruyère Cordon Bleu

**Prep time: 15 minutes | Cook time: 15 minutes | Serves 4**

| | |
|---|---|
| 4 chicken breast filets | Freshly ground black pepper, to taste |
| 75 g chopped ham | |
| 75 g grated Swiss cheese, or Gruyère cheese | ½ teaspoon dried marjoram |
| 30 g all-purpose flour | 1 egg |
| Pinch salt | 120 g panko bread crumbs |
| | Olive oil spray |

1. Put the chicken breast filets on a work surface and gently press them with the palm of your hand to make them a bit thinner. Don't tear the meat. 2. In a small bowl, combine the ham and cheese. Divide this mixture among the chicken filets. Wrap the chicken around the filling to enclose it, using toothpicks to hold the chicken together. 3. In a shallow bowl, stir together the flour, salt, pepper, and marjoram. 4. In another bowl, beat the egg. 5. Spread the panko on a plate. 6. Dip the chicken in the flour mixture, in the egg, and in the panko to coat thoroughly. Press the crumbs into the chicken so they stick well. 7. Insert the crisper plate into the basket and the basket into the unit. Preheat the unit by selecting BAKE, setting the temperature to 190ºC, and setting the time to 3 minutes. Select START/STOP to begin. 8. Once the unit is preheated, spray the crisper plate with olive oil. Place the chicken into the basket and spray it with olive oil. 9. Select BAKE, set the temperature to 190ºC, and set the time to 15 minutes. Select START/STOP to begin. 10. When the cooking is complete, the chicken should be cooked through and a food thermometer inserted into the chicken should register 75ºC. Carefully remove the toothpicks and serve.

## Barbecued Chicken with Creamy Coleslaw

**Prep time: 10 minutes | Cook time: 20 minutes | Serves 2**

| | |
|---|---|
| 270 g shredded coleslaw mix | plus extra for serving |
| Salt and pepper | 2 tablespoons mayonnaise |
| 2 (340 g) bone-in split chicken breasts, trimmed | 2 tablespoons sour cream |
| 1 teaspoon vegetable oil | 1 teaspoon distilled white vinegar, plus extra for seasoning |
| 2 tablespoons barbecue sauce, | ¼ teaspoon sugar |

1. Preheat the air fryer to 180ºC. 2. Toss coleslaw mix and ¼ teaspoon salt in a colander set over bowl. Let sit until wilted slightly, about 30 minutes. Rinse, drain, and dry well with a dish towel. 3. Meanwhile, pat chicken dry with paper towels, rub with oil, and season with salt and pepper. Arrange breasts skin-side down in air fryer basket, spaced evenly apart, alternating ends. Bake for 10 minutes. Flip breasts and brush skin side with barbecue sauce. Return basket to air fryer and bake until well browned and chicken registers 70ºC, 10 to 15 minutes. 4. Transfer chicken to serving platter, tent loosely with aluminum foil, and let rest for 5 minutes. While chicken rests, whisk mayonnaise, sour cream, vinegar, sugar, and pinch pepper together in a large bowl. Stir in coleslaw mix and season with salt, pepper, and additional vinegar to taste. Serve chicken with coleslaw, passing extra barbecue sauce separately.

## Lemon Chicken with Garlic

**Prep time: 5 minutes | Cook time: 20 to 25 minutes | Serves 4**

| | |
|---|---|
| 8 bone-in chicken thighs, skin on | ½ teaspoon paprika |
| | ½ teaspoon garlic powder |
| 1 tablespoon olive oil | ¼ teaspoon freshly ground black pepper |
| 1½ teaspoons lemon-pepper seasoning | |
| | Juice of ½ lemon |

1. Preheat the air fryer to 180ºC. 2. Place the chicken in a large bowl and drizzle with the olive oil. Top with the lemon-pepper seasoning, paprika, garlic powder, and freshly ground black pepper. Toss until thoroughly coated. 3. Working in batches if necessary, arrange the chicken in a single layer in the basket of the air fryer. Pausing halfway through the cooking time to turn the chicken, air fry for 20 to 25 minutes, until a thermometer inserted into the thickest piece registers 75ºC. 4. Transfer the chicken to a serving platter and squeeze the lemon juice over the top.

## Chicken Manchurian

**Prep time: 10 minutes | Cook time: 20 minutes | Serves 2**

| | |
|---|---|
| 450 g boneless, skinless chicken breasts, cut into 1-inch pieces | 2 teaspoons vegetable oil |
| 60 g ketchup | 1 teaspoon hot sauce, such as Tabasco |
| 1 tablespoon tomato-based chili sauce, such as Heinz | ½ teaspoon garlic powder |
| 1 tablespoon soy sauce | ¼ teaspoon cayenne pepper |
| 1 tablespoon rice vinegar | 2 spring onions, thinly sliced |
| | Cooked white rice, for serving |

1. Preheat the air fryer to 180ºC. 2. In a bowl, combine the chicken, ketchup, chili sauce, soy sauce, vinegar, oil, hot sauce, garlic powder, cayenne, and three-quarters of the spring onions and toss until evenly coated. 3. Scrape the chicken and sauce into a metal cake pan and place the pan in the air fryer. Bake until the chicken is cooked through and the sauce is reduced to a thick glaze, about 20 minutes, flipping the chicken pieces halfway through. 4. Remove the pan from the air fryer. Spoon the chicken and sauce over rice and top with the remaining spring onions. Serve immediately.

## Chicken and Vegetable Fajitas

**Prep time: 15 minutes | Cook time: 23 minutes | Serves 6**

| | |
|---|---|
| Chicken: | 1 tablespoon vegetable oil |
| 450 g boneless, skinless chicken thighs, cut crosswise into thirds | ½ teaspoon kosher salt |
| 1 tablespoon vegetable oil | ½ teaspoon ground cumin |
| 4½ teaspoons taco seasoning | For Serving: |
| Vegetables: | Tortillas |
| 50 g sliced onion | Sour cream |
| 150 g sliced bell pepper | Shredded cheese |
| 1 or 2 jalapeños, quartered lengthwise | Guacamole |
| | Salsa |

1. For the chicken: In a medium bowl, toss together the chicken, vegetable oil, and taco seasoning to coat. 2. For the vegetables: In a separate bowl, toss together the onion, bell pepper, jalapeño(s), vegetable oil, salt, and cumin to coat. 3. Place the chicken in the air fryer basket. Set the air fryer to (190ºC for 10 minutes. Add the vegetables to the basket, toss everything together to blend the seasonings, and set the air fryer for 13 minutes more. Use a meat thermometer to ensure the chicken has reached an internal temperature of 75ºC. 4. Transfer the chicken and vegetables to a serving platter. Serve with tortillas and the desired fajita fixings.

## Easy Turkey Tenderloin

**Prep time: 20 minutes | Cook time: 30 minutes | Serves 4**

| | |
|---|---|
| Olive oil | ½ teaspoon freshly ground black pepper |
| ½ teaspoon paprika | Pinch cayenne pepper |
| ½ teaspoon garlic powder | 680 g turkey breast tenderloin |
| ½ teaspoon salt | |

1. Spray the air fryer basket lightly with olive oil. 2. In a small bowl, combine the paprika, garlic powder, salt, black pepper, and cayenne pepper. Rub the mixture all over the turkey. 3. Place the turkey in the air fryer basket and lightly spray with olive oil. 4. Air fry at 190ºC for 15 minutes. Flip the turkey over and lightly spray with olive oil. Air fry until the internal temperature reaches at least 80ºC for an additional 10 to 15 minutes. 5. Let the turkey rest for 10 minutes before slicing and serving.

## Homemade Chicken Jalfrezi

**Prep time: 15 minutes | Cook time: 15 minutes | Serves 4**

| | |
|---|---|
| Chicken: | 1 teaspoon kosher salt |
| 450 g boneless, skinless chicken thighs, cut into 2 or 3 pieces each | ½ to 1 teaspoon cayenne pepper |
| | Sauce: |
| 1 medium onion, chopped | 55 g tomato sauce |
| 1 large green bell pepper, stemmed, seeded, and chopped | 1 tablespoon water |
| | 1 teaspoon garam masala |
| 2 tablespoons olive oil | ½ teaspoon kosher salt |
| 1 teaspoon ground turmeric | ½ teaspoon cayenne pepper |
| 1 teaspoon garam masala | Side salad, rice, or naan bread, for serving |

1. For the chicken: In a large bowl, combine the chicken, onion, bell pepper, oil, turmeric, garam masala, salt, and cayenne. Stir and toss until well combined. 2. Place the chicken and vegetables in the air fryer basket. Set the air fryer to 180ºC for 15 minutes, stirring and tossing halfway through the cooking time. Use a meat thermometer to ensure the chicken has reached an internal temperature of 75ºC. 3. Meanwhile, for the sauce: In a small microwave-safe bowl, combine the tomato sauce, water, garam masala, salt, and cayenne. Microwave on high for 1 minute. Remove and stir. Microwave for another minute; set aside. 4. When the chicken is cooked, remove and place chicken and vegetables in a large bowl. Pour the sauce over all. Stir and toss to coat the chicken and vegetables evenly. 5. Serve with rice, naan, or a side salad.

## Piri-Piri Chicken Thighs

**Prep time: 5 minutes | Cook time: 25 minutes | Serves 4**

| | |
|---|---|
| 60 ml piri-piri sauce | 1 tablespoon extra-virgin olive oil |
| 1 tablespoon freshly squeezed lemon juice | |
| 2 tablespoons brown sugar, divided | 4 bone-in, skin-on chicken thighs, each weighing approximately 200 to 230 g |
| 2 cloves garlic, minced | ½ teaspoon cornflour |

1. To make the marinade, whisk together the piri-piri sauce, lemon juice, 1 tablespoon of brown sugar, and the garlic in a small bowl. While whisking, slowly pour in the oil in a steady stream and continue to whisk until emulsified. Using a skewer, poke holes in the chicken thighs and place them in a small glass dish. Pour the marinade over the chicken and turn the thighs to coat them with the sauce. Cover the dish and refrigerate for at least 15 minutes and up to 1 hour. 2. Preheat the air fryer to 190ºC. Remove the chicken thighs from the dish, reserving the marinade, and place them skin-side down in the air fryer basket. Air fry until the internal temperature reaches 75ºC, 15 to 20 minutes. 3. Meanwhile, whisk the remaining brown sugar and the cornflour into the marinade and microwave it on high power for 1 minute until it is bubbling and thickened to a glaze. 4. Once the chicken is cooked, turn the thighs over and brush them with the glaze. Air fry for a few additional minutes until the glaze browns and begins to char in spots. 5. Remove the chicken to a platter and serve with additional piri-piri sauce, if desired.

## Jalapeño Popper Hasselback Chicken

**Prep time: 10 minutes | Cook time: 19 minutes | Serves 2**

| | |
|---|---|
| Oil, for spraying | 55 g bacon bits |
| 2 (230 g) boneless, skinless chicken breasts | 20 g chopped pickled jalapeños |
| 60 g cream cheese, softened | 40 g shredded Cheddar cheese, divided |

1. Line the air fryer basket with parchment and spray lightly with oil. 2. Make multiple cuts across the top of each chicken breast, cutting only halfway through. 3. In a medium bowl, mix together the cream cheese, bacon bits, jalapeños, and Cheddar cheese. Spoon some of the mixture into each cut. 4. Place the chicken in the prepared basket. 5. Air fry at 175ºC for 14 minutes. Scatter the remaining cheese on top of the chicken and cook for another 2 to 5 minutes, or until the cheese is melted and the internal temperature reaches 75ºC.

## Golden Tenders

**Prep time: 10 minutes | Cook time: 15 minutes | Serves 4**

| | |
|---|---|
| 120 g panko bread crumbs | black pepper |
| 1 tablespoon paprika | 16 chicken tenders |
| ½ teaspoon salt | 115 g mayonnaise |
| ¼ teaspoon freshly ground | Olive oil spray |

1. In a medium bowl, stir together the panko, paprika, salt, and pepper. 2. In a large bowl, toss together the chicken tenders and mayonnaise to coat. Transfer the coated chicken pieces to the bowl of seasoned panko and dredge to coat thoroughly. Press the coating onto the chicken with your fingers. 3. Insert the crisper plate into the basket and the basket into the unit. Preheat the unit by selecting AIR FRY, setting the temperature to 180ºC, and setting the time to 3 minutes. Select START/STOP to begin. 4. Once the unit is preheated, place a parchment paper liner into the basket. Place the chicken into the basket and spray it with olive oil. 5. Select AIR FRY, set the temperature to 180ºC, and set the time to 15 minutes. Select START/STOP to begin. 6. When the cooking is complete, the tenders will be golden brown and a food thermometer inserted into the chicken should register 75ºC. For more even browning, remove the basket halfway through cooking and flip the tenders. Give them an extra spray of olive oil and reinsert the basket to resume cooking. This ensures they are crispy and brown all over. 7. When the cooking is complete, serve.

## Blackened Chicken

**Prep time: 10 minutes | Cook time: 20 minutes | Serves 4**

| | |
|---|---|
| 1 large egg, beaten | chicken breasts (about 450 g each), halved |
| 215 g Blackened seasoning | |
| 2 whole boneless, skinless | 1 to 2 tablespoons oil |

1. Place the beaten egg in one shallow bowl and the Blackened seasoning in another shallow bowl. 2. One at a time, dip the chicken pieces in the beaten egg and the Blackened seasoning, coating thoroughly. 3. Preheat the air fryer to 180ºC. Line the air fryer basket with parchment paper. 4. Place the chicken pieces on the parchment and spritz with oil. 5. Cook for 10 minutes. Flip the chicken, spritz it with oil, and cook for 10 minutes more until the internal temperature reaches 75ºC and the chicken is no longer pink inside. Let sit for 5 minutes before serving.

## Buttermilk-Fried Drumsticks

**Prep time: 10 minutes | Cook time: 25 minutes | Serves 2**

| | |
|---|---|
| 1 egg | 1 teaspoon salt |
| 120 g buttermilk | ¼ teaspoon ground black |
| 90 g self-rising flour | pepper (to mix into coating) |
| 90 g seasoned panko bread | 4 chicken drumsticks, skin on |
| crumbs | Oil for misting or cooking spray |

1. Beat together egg and buttermilk in shallow dish. 2. In a second shallow dish, combine the flour, panko crumbs, salt, and pepper. 3. Sprinkle chicken legs with additional salt and pepper to taste. 4. Dip legs in buttermilk mixture, then roll in panko mixture, pressing in crumbs to make coating stick. Mist with oil or cooking spray. 5. Spray the air fryer basket with cooking spray. 6. Cook drumsticks at 180ºC for 10 minutes. Turn pieces over and cook an additional 10 minutes. 7. Turn pieces to check for browning. If you have any white spots that haven't begun to brown, spritz them with oil or cooking spray. Continue cooking for 5 more minutes or until crust is golden brown and juices run clear. Larger, meatier drumsticks will take longer to cook than small ones.

## Thai Tacos with Peanut Sauce

**Prep time: 10 minutes | Cook time: 6 minutes | Serves 4**

| | |
|---|---|
| 450 g chicken mince | 2 tablespoons wheat-free tamari |
| 10 g diced onions (about 1 | or coconut aminos |
| small onion) | 1½ teaspoons hot sauce |
| 2 cloves garlic, minced | 5 drops liquid stevia (optional) |
| ¼ teaspoon fine sea salt | For Serving: |
| Sauce: | 2 small heads butter lettuce, |
| 60 g creamy peanut butter, | leaves separated |
| room temperature | Lime slices (optional) |
| 2 tablespoons chicken broth, | For Garnish (Optional): |
| plus more if needed | Coriander leaves |
| 2 tablespoons lime juice | Shredded purple cabbage |
| 2 tablespoons grated fresh | Sliced green onions |
| ginger | |

1. Preheat the air fryer to 180ºC. . 2. Place the chicken mince, onions, garlic, and salt in a pie pan or a dish that will fit in your air fryer. Break up the chicken with a spatula. Place in the air fryer and bake for 5 minutes, or until the chicken is browned and cooked through. Break up the chicken again into small crumbles. 3. Make the sauce: In a medium-sized bowl, stir together the peanut butter, broth, lime juice, ginger, tamari, hot sauce, and stevia (if using) until well combined. If the sauce is too thick, add another tablespoon or two of broth. Taste and add more hot sauce if desired. 4. Add half of the sauce to the pan with the chicken. Cook for another minute, until heated through, and stir well to combine. 5. Assemble the tacos: Place several lettuce leaves on a serving plate. Place a few tablespoons of the chicken mixture in each lettuce leaf and garnish with coriander leaves, purple cabbage, and sliced green onions, if desired. Serve the remaining sauce on the side. Serve with lime slices, if desired. 6. Store leftover meat mixture in an airtight container in the refrigerator for up to 4 days; store leftover sauce, lettuce leaves, and garnishes separately. Reheat the meat mixture in a lightly greased pie pan in a preheated 180ºC air fryer for 3 minutes, or until heated through.

## Air Fried Chicken Potatoes with Sun-Dried Tomato

**Prep time: 15 minutes | Cook time: 25 minutes | Serves 2**

| | |
|---|---|
| 2 teaspoons minced fresh | 15 g oil-packed sun-dried |
| oregano, divided | tomatoes, patted dry and |
| 2 teaspoons minced fresh | chopped |
| thyme, divided | 1½ tablespoons red wine |
| 2 teaspoons extra-virgin olive | vinegar |
| oil, plus extra as needed | 1 tablespoon capers, rinsed and |
| 450 g fingerling potatoes, | minced |
| unpeeled | 1 small shallot, minced |
| 2 (340 g) bone-in split chicken | Salt and ground black pepper, |
| breasts, trimmed | to taste |
| 1 garlic clove, minced | |

1. Preheat the air fryer to 180ºC. 2. Combine 1 teaspoon of oregano, 1 teaspoon of thyme, ¼ teaspoon of salt, ¼ teaspoon of ground black pepper, 1 teaspoons of olive oil in a large bowl. Add the potatoes and toss to coat well. 3. Combine the chicken with remaining thyme, oregano, and olive oil. Sprinkle with garlic, salt, and pepper. Toss to coat well. 4. Place the potatoes in the preheated air fryer, then arrange the chicken on top of the potatoes. 5. Air fry for 25 minutes or until the internal temperature of the chicken reaches at least 75ºC and the potatoes are wilted. Flip the chicken and potatoes halfway through. 6. Meanwhile, combine the sun-dried tomatoes, vinegar, capers, and shallot in a separate large bowl. Sprinkle with salt and ground black pepper. Toss to mix well. 7. Remove the chicken and potatoes from the air fryer and allow to cool for 10 minutes. Serve with the sun-dried tomato mix.

## Classic Chicken Kebab

**Prep time: 35 minutes | Cook time: 25 minutes | Serves 4**

60 ml olive oil

1 teaspoon garlic powder

1 teaspoon onion powder

1 teaspoon ground cumin

½ teaspoon dried oregano

½ teaspoon dried basil

60 ml lemon juice

1 tablespoon apple cider vinegar

Olive oil cooking spray

450 g boneless skinless chicken thighs, cut into 1-inch pieces

1 red bell pepper, cut into 1-inch pieces

1 red onion, cut into 1-inch pieces

1 courgette, cut into 1-inch pieces

12 cherry tomatoes

1. In a large bowl, mix together the olive oil, garlic powder, onion powder, cumin, oregano, basil, lemon juice, and apple cider vinegar. 2. Spray six skewers with olive oil cooking spray. 3. On each skewer, slide on a piece of chicken, then a piece of bell pepper, onion, courgette, and finally a tomato and then repeat. Each skewer should have at least two pieces of each item. 4. Once all of the skewers are prepared, place them in a 9-by-13-inch baking dish and pour the olive oil marinade over the top of the skewers. Turn each skewer so that all sides of the chicken and vegetables are coated. 5. Cover the dish with plastic wrap and place it in the refrigerator for 30 minutes. 6. After 30 minutes, preheat the air fryer to 190ºC. (If using a grill attachment, make sure it is inside the air fryer during preheating.) 7. Remove the skewers from the marinade and lay them in a single layer in the air fryer basket. If the air fryer has a grill attachment, you can also lay them on this instead. 8. Cook for 10 minutes. Rotate the kebabs, then cook them for 15 minutes more. 9. Remove the skewers from the air fryer and let them rest for 5 minutes before serving.

## Apricot-Glazed Chicken Drumsticks

**Prep time: 15 minutes | Cook time: 30 minutes | Makes 6 drumsticks**

For the Glaze:

160 g apricot preserves

½ teaspoon tamari

¼ teaspoon chili powder

2 teaspoons Dijon mustard

For the Chicken:

6 chicken drumsticks

½ teaspoon seasoning salt

1 teaspoon salt

½ teaspoon ground black pepper

Cooking spray

Make the glaze: 1. Combine the ingredients for the glaze in a saucepan, then heat over low heat for 10 minutes or until thickened.

2. Turn off the heat and sit until ready to use. Make the Chicken: 1. Preheat the air fryer to 190ºC. Spritz the air fryer basket with cooking spray. 2. Combine the seasoning salt, salt, and pepper in a small bowl. Stir to mix well. 3. Place the chicken drumsticks in the preheated air fryer. Spritz with cooking spray and sprinkle with the salt mixture on both sides. 4. Air fry for 20 minutes or until well browned. Flip the chicken halfway through. 5. Baste the chicken with the glaze and air fryer for 2 more minutes or until the chicken tenderloin is glossy. 6. Serve immediately.

## Chicken Nuggets

**Prep time: 10 minutes | Cook time: 15 minutes | Serves 4**

450 g chicken mince thighs

110 g shredded Mozzarella cheese

1 large egg, whisked

½ teaspoon salt

¼ teaspoon dried oregano

¼ teaspoon garlic powder

1. In a large bowl, combine all ingredients. Form mixture into twenty nugget shapes, about 2 tablespoons each. 2. Place nuggets into ungreased air fryer basket, working in batches if needed. Adjust the temperature to (190ºC and air fry for 15 minutes, turning nuggets halfway through cooking. Let cool 5 minutes before serving.

## Chicken Wings with Piri Piri Sauce

**Prep time: 30 minutes | Cook time: 30 minutes | Serves 6**

12 chicken wings

45 g butter, melted

1 teaspoon onion powder

½ teaspoon cumin powder

1 teaspoon garlic paste

Sauce:

60 g piri piri peppers, stemmed

and chopped

1 tablespoon pimiento, seeded and minced

1 garlic clove, chopped

2 tablespoons fresh lemon juice

⅓ teaspoon sea salt

½ teaspoon tarragon

1. Steam the chicken wings using a steamer basket that is placed over a saucepan with boiling water; reduce the heat. 2. Now, steam the wings for 10 minutes over a moderate heat. Toss the wings with butter, onion powder, cumin powder, and garlic paste. 3. Let the chicken wings cool to room temperature. Then, refrigerate them for 45 to 50 minutes. 4. Roast in the preheated air fryer at 170ºC for 25 to 30 minutes; make sure to flip them halfway through. 5. While the chicken wings are cooking, prepare the sauce by mixing all of the sauce ingredients in a food processor. Toss the wings with prepared Piri Piri Sauce and serve.

## Seasoned Chicken Drumsticks with Barbecue Sauce

**Prep time: 5 minutes | Cook time: 40 minutes | Serves 5**

| | |
|---|---|
| 1 tablespoon olive oil | Salt and ground black pepper, |
| 10 chicken drumsticks | to taste |
| Chicken seasoning or rub, to | 240 ml barbecue sauce |
| taste | 85 g honey |

1. Preheat the air fryer to 200ºC. Grease the air fryer basket with olive oil. 2. Rub the chicken drumsticks with chicken seasoning or rub, salt and ground black pepper on a clean work surface. 3. Arrange the chicken drumsticks in a single layer in the air fryer, then air fry for 18 minutes or until lightly browned. Flip the drumsticks halfway through. You may need to work in batches to avoid overcrowding. 4. Meanwhile, combine the barbecue sauce and honey in a small bowl. Stir to mix well. 5. Remove the drumsticks from the air fryer and baste with the sauce mixture to serve.

## Italian Crispy Chicken

**Prep time: 10 minutes | Cook time: 20 minutes | Serves 4**

| | |
|---|---|
| 2 (115 g) boneless, skinless | Salt and freshly ground black |
| chicken breasts | pepper, to taste |
| 2 egg whites, beaten | Cooking oil spray |
| 120 g Italian bread crumbs | 180 g marinara sauce |
| 45 g grated Parmesan cheese | 110 g shredded Mozzarella |
| 2 teaspoons Italian seasoning | cheese |

1. With your knife blade parallel to the cutting board, cut the chicken breasts in half horizontally to create 4 thin cutlets. On a solid surface, pound the cutlets to flatten them. You can use your hands, a rolling pin, a kitchen mallet, or a meat hammer. 2. Pour the egg whites into a bowl large enough to dip the chicken. 3. In another bowl large enough to dip a chicken cutlet in, stir together the bread crumbs, Parmesan cheese, and Italian seasoning, and season with salt and pepper. 4. Dip each cutlet into the egg whites and into the breadcrumb mixture to coat. 5. Insert the crisper plate into the basket and the basket into the unit. Preheat the unit by selecting AIR FRY, setting the temperature to 190ºC, and setting the time to 3 minutes. Select START/STOP to begin. 6. Once the unit is preheated, spray the crisper plate with cooking oil. Working in batches, place 2 chicken cutlets into the basket. Spray the top of the chicken with cooking oil. 7. Select AIR FRY, set the temperature to 190ºC, and set the time to 7 minutes. Select START/STOP to begin. 8. When the cooking is complete, repeat steps 6 and 7 with the remaining cutlets. 9. Top the chicken cutlets with the marinara sauce and shredded Mozzarella cheese. If the chicken will fit into the basket without stacking, you can prepare all 4 at once. Otherwise, do this 2 cutlets at a time. 10. Select AIR FRY, set the temperature to 190ºC, and set the time to 3 minutes. Select START/STOP to begin. 11. The cooking is complete when the cheese is melted and the chicken reaches an internal temperature of 75ºC. Cool for 5 minutes before serving.

## Chicken Strips with Satay Sauce

**Prep time: 15 minutes | Cook time: 10 minutes | Serves 4**

| | |
|---|---|
| 4 (170 g) boneless, skinless | fresh ginger |
| chicken breasts, sliced into 16 | ½ teaspoon hot sauce |
| (1-inch) strips | ⅛ teaspoon stevia glycerite, or |
| 1 teaspoon fine sea salt | 2 to 3 drops liquid stevia |
| 1 teaspoon paprika | For Garnish/Serving (Optional): |
| Sauce: | 15 g chopped coriander leaves |
| 60 g creamy almond butter (or | Red pepper flakes |
| sunflower seed butter for nut- | Sea salt flakes |
| free) | Thinly sliced red, orange, and |
| 2 tablespoons chicken broth | yellow bell peppers |
| 1½ tablespoons coconut vinegar | Special Equipment: |
| or unseasoned rice vinegar | 16 wooden or bamboo skewers, |
| 1 clove garlic, minced | soaked in water for 15 minutes |
| 1 teaspoon peeled and minced | |

1. Spray the air fryer basket with avocado oil. Preheat the air fryer to 200ºC. 2. Thread the chicken strips onto the skewers. Season on all sides with the salt and paprika. Place the chicken skewers in the air fryer basket and air fry for 5 minutes, flip, and cook for another 5 minutes, until the chicken is cooked through and the internal temperature reaches 75ºC. 3. While the chicken skewers cook, make the sauce: In a medium-sized bowl, stir together all the sauce ingredients until well combined. Taste and adjust the sweetness and heat to your liking. 4. Garnish the chicken with coriander, red pepper flakes, and salt flakes, if desired, and serve with sliced bell peppers, if desired. Serve the sauce on the side. 5. Store leftovers in an airtight container in the fridge for up to 4 days or in the freezer for up to a month. Reheat in a preheated 180ºC air fryer for 3 minutes per side, or until heated through.

## Cheesy Pepperoni and Chicken Pizza

**Prep time: 15 minutes | Cook time: 15 minutes | Serves 6**

280 g cooked chicken, cubed
240 g pizza sauce
20 slices pepperoni

20 g grated Parmesan cheese
225 g shredded Mozzarella cheese
Cooking spray

1. Preheat the air fryer to 190ºC. Spritz a baking pan with cooking spray. 2. Arrange the chicken cubes in the prepared baking pan, then top the cubes with pizza sauce and pepperoni. Stir to coat the cubes and pepperoni with sauce. 3. Scatter the cheeses on top, then place the baking pan in the preheated air fryer. Air fryer for 15 minutes or until frothy and the cheeses melt. 4. Serve immediately.

## Teriyaki Chicken Legs

**Prep time: 12 minutes | Cook time: 18 to 20 minutes | Serves 2**

4 tablespoons teriyaki sauce
1 tablespoon orange juice
1 teaspoon smoked paprika

4 chicken legs
Cooking spray

1. Mix together the teriyaki sauce, orange juice, and smoked paprika. Brush on all sides of chicken legs. 2. Spray the air fryer basket with nonstick cooking spray and place chicken in basket. 3. Air fry at 180ºC for 6 minutes. Turn and baste with sauce. Cook for 6 more minutes, turn and baste. Cook for 6 to 8 minutes more, until juices run clear when chicken is pierced with a fork.

## Spicy Chicken Thighs and Gold Potatoes

**Prep time: 5 minutes | Cook time: 25 minutes | Serves 4**

4 bone-in, skin-on chicken thighs
½ teaspoon kosher salt or ¼ teaspoon fine salt
2 tablespoons melted unsalted butter
2 teaspoons Worcestershire sauce
2 teaspoons curry powder

1 teaspoon dried oregano leaves
½ teaspoon dry mustard
½ teaspoon granulated garlic
¼ teaspoon paprika
¼ teaspoon hot pepper sauce
Cooking oil spray
4 medium Yukon gold potatoes, chopped
1 tablespoon extra-virgin olive oil

1. Sprinkle the chicken thighs on both sides with salt. 2. In a medium bowl, stir together the melted butter, Worcestershire sauce, curry powder, oregano, dry mustard, granulated garlic, paprika, and hot pepper sauce. Add the thighs to the sauce and stir to coat. 3. Insert the crisper plate into the basket and the basket into the unit. Preheat the unit by selecting AIR FRY, setting the temperature to 200ºC, and setting the time to 3 minutes. Select START/STOP to begin. 4. Once the unit is preheated, spray the crisper plate with cooking oil. In the basket, combine the potatoes and olive oil and toss to coat. 5. Add the wire rack to the air fryer and place the chicken thighs on top. 6. Select AIR FRY, set the temperature to 200ºC, and set the time to 25 minutes. Select START/STOP to begin. 7. After 19 minutes check the chicken thighs. If a food thermometer inserted into the chicken registers 75ºC, transfer them to a clean plate, and cover with aluminum foil to keep warm. If they aren't cooked to 75ºC, resume cooking for another 1 to 2 minutes until they are done. Remove them from the unit along with the rack. 8. Remove the basket and shake it to distribute the potatoes. Reinsert the basket to resume cooking for 3 to 6 minutes, or until the potatoes are crisp and golden brown. 9. When the cooking is complete, serve the chicken with the potatoes.

## African Merguez Meatballs

**Prep time: 30 minutes | Cook time: 10 minutes | Serves 4**

450 g chicken mince
2 garlic cloves, finely minced
1 tablespoon sweet Hungarian paprika
1 teaspoon kosher salt
1 teaspoon sugar

1 teaspoon ground cumin
½ teaspoon black pepper
½ teaspoon ground fennel
½ teaspoon ground coriander
½ teaspoon cayenne pepper
¼ teaspoon ground allspice

1. In a large bowl, gently mix the chicken, garlic, paprika, salt, sugar, cumin, black pepper, fennel, coriander, cayenne, and allspice until all the ingredients are incorporated. Let stand for 30 minutes at room temperature, or cover and refrigerate for up to 24 hours. 2. Form the mixture into 16 meatballs. Arrange them in a single layer in the air fryer basket. Set the air fryer to 200ºC for 10 minutes, turning the meatballs halfway through the cooking time. Use a meat thermometer to ensure the meatballs have reached an internal temperature of 75ºC.

## Chipotle Drumsticks

**Prep time: 15 minutes | Cook time: 20 minutes | Serves 4**

1 tablespoon tomato paste
½ teaspoon chipotle powder
¼ teaspoon apple cider vinegar
¼ teaspoon garlic powder

8 chicken drumsticks
½ teaspoon salt
⅛ teaspoon ground black pepper

1. In a small bowl, combine tomato paste, chipotle powder, vinegar, and garlic powder. 2. Sprinkle drumsticks with salt and pepper, then place into a large bowl and pour in tomato paste mixture. Toss or stir to evenly coat all drumsticks in mixture. 3. Place drumsticks into ungreased air fryer basket. Adjust the temperature to 200ºC and air fry for 25 minutes, turning drumsticks halfway through cooking. Drumsticks will be dark red with an internal temperature of at least 75ºC when done. Serve warm.

# Chapter 6 Beef, Pork, and Lamb

# Chapter 6 Beef, Pork, and Lamb

## Steaks with Walnut-Blue Cheese Butter

**Prep time: 30 minutes | Cook time: 10 minutes | Serves 6**

120 ml unsalted butter, at room temperature

120 ml crumbled blue cheese

2 tablespoons finely chopped walnuts

1 tablespoon minced fresh rosemary

1 teaspoon minced garlic

¼ teaspoon cayenne pepper

Sea salt and freshly ground black pepper, to taste

680 g sirloin steaks, at room temperature

1. In a medium bowl, combine the butter, blue cheese, walnuts, rosemary, garlic, and cayenne pepper and salt and black pepper to taste. Use clean hands to ensure that everything is well combined. Place the mixture on a sheet of parchment paper and form it into a log. Wrap it tightly in plastic wrap. Refrigerate for at least 2 hours or freeze for 30 minutes. 2. Season the steaks generously with salt and pepper. 3. Place the air fryer basket or grill pan in the air fryer. Set the air fryer to 200ºC and let it preheat for 5 minutes. 4. Place the steaks in the basket in a single layer and air fry for 5 minutes. Flip the steaks, and cook for 5 minutes more, until an instant-read thermometer reads 50ºC for medium-rare (or as desired). 5. Transfer the steaks to a plate. Cut the butter into pieces and place the desired amount on top of the steaks. Tent a piece of aluminum foil over the steaks and allow to sit for 10 minutes before serving. 6. Store any remaining butter in a sealed container in the refrigerator for up to 2 weeks.

## Bo Luc Lac

**Prep time: 50 minutes | Cook time: 8 minutes | Serves 4**

For the Meat:

2 teaspoons soy sauce

4 garlic cloves, minced

1 teaspoon coarse or flaky salt

2 teaspoons sugar

¼ teaspoon ground black pepper

1 teaspoon toasted sesame oil

680 g top rump steak, cut into 1-inch cubes

Cooking spray

For the Salad:

1 head butterhead lettuce, leaves separated and torn into large pieces

60 ml fresh mint leaves

120 ml halved baby plum tomatoes

½ red onion, halved and thinly sliced

2 tablespoons apple cider vinegar

1 garlic clove, minced

2 teaspoons sugar

¼ teaspoon coarse or flaky salt

¼ teaspoon ground black pepper

2 tablespoons vegetable oil

For Serving:

Lime wedges, for garnish

Coarse salt and freshly cracked black pepper, to taste

1. Combine the ingredients for the meat, except for the steak, in a large bowl. Stir to mix well. 2. Dunk the steak cubes in the bowl and press to coat. Wrap the bowl in plastic and marinate under room temperature for at least 30 minutes. 3. Preheat the air fryer to 230ºC. Spritz the air fryer basket with cooking spray. 4. Discard the marinade and transfer the steak cubes in the preheated air fryer basket. You need to air fry in batches to avoid overcrowding. 5. Air fry for 4 minutes or until the steak cubes are lightly browned but still have a little pink. Shake the basket halfway through the cooking time. 6. Meanwhile, combine the ingredients for the salad in a separate large bowl. Toss to mix well. 7. Pour the salad in a large serving bowl and top with the steak cubes. Squeeze the lime wedges over and sprinkle with salt and black pepper before serving.

## Beef and Pork Sausage Meatloaf

**Prep time: 20 minutes | Cook time: 25 minutes | Serves 4**

340 g beef mince

110 g pork sausage meat

235 ml shallots, finely chopped

2 eggs, well beaten

3 tablespoons milk

1 tablespoon oyster sauce

1 teaspoon porcini mushrooms

½ teaspoon cumin powder

1 teaspoon garlic paste

1 tablespoon fresh parsley

Salt and crushed red pepper flakes, to taste

235 ml crushed cream crackers

Cooking spray

1. Preheat the air fryer to 180ºC. Spritz a baking dish with cooking spray. 2. Mix all the ingredients in a large bowl, combining everything well. 3. Transfer to the baking dish and bake in the air fryer for 25 minutes. 4. Serve hot.

## Beef and Spinach Rolls

**Prep time: 10 minutes | Cook time: 14 minutes | Serves 2**

| | |
|---|---|
| 3 teaspoons pesto | 85 g roasted red peppers |
| 900 g beef bavette or skirt steak | 180 ml baby spinach |
| 6 slices low-moisture Mozarella or other melting cheese | 1 teaspoon sea salt |
| | 1 teaspoon black pepper |

1. Preheat the air fryer to 200ºC. 2. Spoon equal amounts of the pesto onto each steak and spread it across evenly. 3. Put the cheese, roasted red peppers and spinach on top of the meat, about three-quarters of the way down. 4. Roll the steak up, holding it in place with toothpicks. Sprinkle with the sea salt and pepper. 5. Put inside the air fryer and air fry for 14 minutes, turning halfway through the cooking time. 6. Allow the beef to rest for 10 minutes before slicing up and serving.

## Steak with Bell Pepper

**Prep time: 30 minutes | Cook time: 20 to 23 minutes | Serves 6**

| | |
|---|---|
| 60 ml avocado oil | 450 g top rump steak or bavette or skirt steak, thinly sliced against the grain |
| 60 ml freshly squeezed lime juice | |
| 2 teaspoons minced garlic | 1 red pepper, cored, seeded, and cut into ½-inch slices |
| 1 tablespoon chili powder | |
| ½ teaspoon ground cumin | 1 green pepper, cored, seeded, and cut into ½-inch slices |
| Sea salt and freshly ground black pepper, to taste | 1 large onion, sliced |

1. In a small bowl or blender, combine the avocado oil, lime juice, garlic, chili powder, cumin, and salt and pepper to taste. 2. Place the sliced steak in a zip-top bag or shallow dish. Place the peppers and onion in a separate zip-top bag or dish. Pour half the marinade over the steak and the other half over the vegetables. Seal both bags and let the steak and vegetables marinate in the refrigerator for at least 1 hour or up to 4 hours. 3. Line the air fryer basket with an air fryer liner or aluminum foil. Remove the vegetables from their bag or dish and shake off any excess marinade. Set the air fryer to 200ºC. Place the vegetables in the air fryer basket and cook for 13 minutes. 4. Remove the steak from its bag or dish and shake off any excess marinade. Place the steak on top of the vegetables in the air fryer, and cook for 7 to 10 minutes or until an instant-read thermometer reads 50ºC for medium-rare (or cook to your desired doneness). 5. Serve with desired fixings, such as keto tortillas, lettuce, sour cream, avocado slices, shredded Cheddar cheese, and coriander.

## Pork Medallions with Endive Salad

**Prep time: 25 minutes | Cook time: 7 minutes | Serves 4**

| | |
|---|---|
| 1 (230 g) pork tenderloin | honey or maple syrup) |
| Salt and freshly ground black pepper, to taste | 1 tablespoon Dijon mustard |
| | juice of ½ lemon |
| 60 ml flour | 2 tablespoons chopped chervil or flat-leaf parsley |
| 2 eggs, lightly beaten | |
| 180 ml finely crushed crackers | salt and freshly ground black pepper |
| 1 teaspoon paprika | |
| 1 teaspoon mustard powder | 120 ml extra-virgin olive oil |
| 1 teaspoon garlic powder | Endive Salad: |
| 1 teaspoon dried thyme | 1 heart romaine lettuce, torn into large pieces |
| 1 teaspoon salt | |
| vegetable or rapeseed oil, in spray bottle | 2 heads endive, sliced |
| | 120 ml cherry tomatoes, halved |
| Vinaigrette: | 85 g fresh Mozzarella, diced |
| 60 ml white balsamic vinegar | Salt and freshly ground black pepper, to taste |
| 2 tablespoons agave syrup (or | |

1. Slice the pork tenderloin into 1-inch slices. Using a meat pounder, pound the pork slices into thin ½-inch medallions. Generously season the pork with salt and freshly ground black pepper on both sides. 2. Set up a dredging station using three shallow dishes. Put the flour in one dish and the beaten eggs in a second dish. Combine the crushed crackers, paprika, mustard powder, garlic powder, thyme and salt in a third dish. 3. Preheat the air fryer to 200ºC. 4. Dredge the pork medallions in flour first and then into the beaten egg. Let the excess egg drip off and coat both sides of the medallions with the cracker crumb mixture. Spray both sides of the coated medallions with vegetable or rapeseed oil. 5. Air fry the medallions in two batches at 200ºC for 5 minutes. Once you have air-fried all the medallions, flip them all over and return the first batch of medallions back into the air fryer on top of the second batch. Air fry at 200ºC for an additional 2 minutes. 6. While the medallions are cooking, make the salad and dressing. Whisk the white balsamic vinegar, agave syrup, Dijon mustard, lemon juice, chervil, salt and pepper together in a small bowl. Whisk in the olive oil slowly until combined and thickened. 7. Combine the romaine lettuce, endive, cherry tomatoes, and Mozzarella cheese in a large salad bowl. Drizzle the dressing over the vegetables and toss to combine. Season with salt and freshly ground black pepper. 8. Serve the pork medallions warm on or beside the salad.

## Italian Sausage and Cheese Meatballs

**Prep time: 10 minutes | Cook time: 20 minutes | Serves 4**

230 g sausage meat with Italian seasoning added to taste
230 g 85% lean beef mince
120 ml shredded sharp Cheddar
cheese
½ teaspoon onion granules
½ teaspoon garlic powder
½ teaspoon black pepper

1. In a large bowl, gently mix the sausage meat, beef mince, cheese, onion granules, garlic powder, and pepper until well combined. 2. Form the mixture into 16 meatballs. Place the meatballs in a single layer in the air fryer basket. Set the air fryer to 175ºC for 20 minutes, turning the meatballs halfway through the cooking time. Use a meat thermometer to ensure the meatballs have reached an internal temperature of 70ºC (medium).

## Nigerian Peanut-Crusted Bavette Steak

**Prep time: 30 minutes | Cook time: 8 minutes | Serves 4**

Suya Spice Mix:
60 ml dry-roasted peanuts
1 teaspoon cumin seeds
1 teaspoon garlic powder
1 teaspoon smoked paprika
½ teaspoon ground ginger
1 teaspoon coarse or flaky salt
½ teaspoon cayenne pepper
Steak:
450 g bavette or skirt steak
2 tablespoons vegetable oil

1. For the spice mix: In a clean coffee grinder or spice mill, combine the peanuts and cumin seeds. Process until you get a coarse powder. (Do not overprocess or you will wind up with peanut butter! Alternatively, you can grind the cumin with 80 ml ready-made peanut powder instead of the peanuts.) 2. Pour the peanut mixture into a small bowl, add the garlic powder, paprika, ginger, salt, and cayenne, and stir to combine. This recipe makes about 120 ml suya spice mix. Store leftovers in an airtight container in a cool, dry place for up to 1 month. 3. For the steak: Cut the steak into ½-inch-thick slices, cutting against the grain and at a slight angle. Place the beef strips in a resealable plastic bag and add the oil and 2½ to 3 tablespoons of the spice mixture. Seal the bag and massage to coat all of the meat with the oil and spice mixture. Marinate at room temperature for 30 minutes or in the refrigerator for up to 24 hours. 4. Place the beef strips in the air fryer basket. Set the air fryer to 200ºC for 8 minutes, turning the strips halfway through the cooking time. 5. Transfer the meat to a serving platter. Sprinkle with additional spice mix, if desired.

## Spicy Lamb Sirloin Chops

**Prep time: 30 minutes | Cook time: 15 minutes | Serves 4**

½ brown onion, coarsely chopped
4 coin-size slices peeled fresh ginger
5 garlic cloves
1 teaspoon garam masala
1 teaspoon ground fennel
1 teaspoon ground cinnamon
1 teaspoon ground turmeric
½ to 1 teaspoon cayenne pepper
½ teaspoon ground cardamom
1 teaspoon coarse or flaky salt
450 g lamb sirloin chops

1. In a blender, combine the onion, ginger, garlic, garam masala, fennel, cinnamon, turmeric, cayenne, cardamom, and salt. Pulse until the onion is finely minced and the mixture forms a thick paste, 3 to 4 minutes. 2. Place the lamb chops in a large bowl. Slash the meat and fat with a sharp knife several times to allow the marinade to penetrate better. Add the spice paste to the bowl and toss the lamb to coat. Marinate at room temperature for 30 minutes or cover and refrigerate for up to 24 hours. 3. Place the lamb chops in a single layer in the air fryer basket. Set the air fryer to 165ºC for 15 minutes, turning the chops halfway through the cooking time. Use a meat thermometer to ensure the lamb has reached an internal temperature of 65ºC (medium-rare).

## Macadamia Nuts Crusted Pork Rack

**Prep time: 5 minutes | Cook time: 35 minutes | Serves 2**

1 clove garlic, minced
2 tablespoons olive oil
450 g rack of pork
235 ml chopped macadamia nuts
1 tablespoon breadcrumbs
1 tablespoon rosemary, chopped
1 egg
Salt and ground black pepper, to taste

1. Preheat the air fryer to 175ºC. 2. Combine the garlic and olive oil in a small bowl. Stir to mix well. 3. On a clean work surface, rub the pork rack with the garlic oil and sprinkle with salt and black pepper on both sides. 4. Combine the macadamia nuts, breadcrumbs, and rosemary in a shallow dish. Whisk the egg in a large bowl. 5. Dredge the pork in the egg, then roll the pork over the macadamia nut mixture to coat well. Shake the excess off. 6. Arrange the pork in the preheated air fryer and air fry for 30 minutes on both sides. Increase to 200ºC and fry for 5 more minutes or until the pork is well browned. 7. Serve immediately.

## Homemade Smothered Chops

**Prep time: 20 minutes | Cook time: 30 minutes | Serves 4**

| | |
|---|---|
| 4 bone-in pork chops (230 g each) | 1½ teaspoons Italian seasoning |
| 2 teaspoons salt, divided | 1 tablespoon sugar |
| 1½ teaspoons freshly ground black pepper, divided | 1 tablespoon cornflour |
| 1 teaspoon garlic powder | 120 ml chopped onion |
| 235 ml tomato purée | 120 ml chopped green pepper |
| | 1 to 2 tablespoons oil |

1. Evenly season the pork chops with 1 teaspoon salt, 1 teaspoon pepper, and the garlic powder. 2. In a medium bowl, stir together the tomato purée, Italian seasoning, sugar, remaining 1 teaspoon of salt, and remaining ½ teaspoon of pepper. 3. In a small bowl, whisk 180 ml water and the cornflour until blended. Stir this slurry into the tomato purée, with the onion and green pepper. Transfer to a baking pan. 4. Preheat the air fryer to 175ºC. 5. Place the sauce in the fryer and cook for 10 minutes. Stir and cook for 10 minutes more. Remove the pan and keep warm. 6. Increase the air fryer temperature to 200ºC. Line the air fryer basket with parchment paper. 7. Place the pork chops on the parchment and spritz with oil. 8. Cook for 5 minutes. Flip and spritz the chops with oil and cook for 5 minutes more, until the internal temperature reaches 65ºC. Serve with the tomato mixture spooned on top.

## Lemony Pork Loin Chop Schnitzel

**Prep time: 15 minutes | Cook time: 15 minutes | Serves 4**

| | |
|---|---|
| 4 thin boneless pork loin chops | 235 ml panko breadcrumbs |
| 2 tablespoons lemon juice | 2 eggs |
| 120 ml flour | Lemon wedges, for serving |
| ¼ teaspoon marjoram | Cooking spray |
| 1 teaspoon salt | |

1. Preheat the air fryer to 200ºC and spritz with cooking spray. 2. On a clean work surface, drizzle the pork chops with lemon juice on both sides. 3. Combine the flour with marjoram and salt on a shallow plate. Pour the breadcrumbs on a separate shallow dish. Beat the eggs in a large bowl. 4. Dredge the pork chops in the flour, then dunk in the beaten eggs to coat well. Shake the excess off and roll over the breadcrumbs. 5. Arrange the chops in the preheated air fryer and spritz with cooking spray. Air fry for 15 minutes or until the chops are golden and crispy. Flip the chops halfway through. Squeeze the lemon wedges over the fried chops and serve immediately.

## Italian Sausage Links

**Prep time: 10 minutes | Cook time: 24 minutes | Serves 4**

| | |
|---|---|
| 1 pepper (any color), sliced | Sea salt and freshly ground |
| 1 medium onion, sliced | black pepper, to taste |
| 1 tablespoon avocado oil | 450 g Italian-seasoned sausage |
| 1 teaspoon Italian seasoning | links |

1. Place the pepper and onion in a medium bowl, and toss with the avocado oil, Italian seasoning, and salt and pepper to taste. 2. Set the air fryer to 200ºC. Put the vegetables in the air fryer basket and cook for 12 minutes. 3. Push the vegetables to the side of the basket and arrange the sausage links in the bottom of the basket in a single layer. Spoon the vegetables over the sausages. Cook for 12 minutes, tossing halfway through, until an instant-read thermometer inserted into the sausage reads 70ºC.

## Greek Stuffed Fillet

**Prep time: 10 minutes | Cook time: 10 minutes | Serves 4**

| | |
|---|---|
| 680 g venison or beef fillet, pounded to ¼ inch thick | 2 cloves garlic, minced |
| 3 teaspoons fine sea salt | For Garnish/Serving (Optional): |
| 1 teaspoon ground black pepper | Yellow/American mustard |
| 60 g creamy goat cheese | Halved cherry tomatoes |
| 120 ml crumbled feta cheese (about 60 g) | Extra-virgin olive oil |
| 60 ml finely chopped onions | Sprigs of fresh rosemary |
| | Lavender flowers |

1. Spray the air fryer basket with avocado oil. Preheat the air fryer to 200ºC. 2. Season the fillet on all sides with the salt and pepper. 3. In a medium-sized mixing bowl, combine the goat cheese, feta, onions, and garlic. Place the mixture in the center of the tenderloin. Starting at the end closest to you, tightly roll the tenderloin like a jelly roll. Tie the rolled tenderloin tightly with kitchen twine. 4. Place the meat in the air fryer basket and air fry for 5 minutes. Flip the meat over and cook for another 5 minutes, or until the internal temperature reaches 60ºC for medium-rare. 5. To serve, smear a line of yellow mustard on a platter, then place the meat next to it and add halved cherry tomatoes on the side, if desired. Drizzle with olive oil and garnish with rosemary sprigs and lavender flowers, if desired. 6. Best served fresh. Store leftovers in an airtight container in the fridge for 3 days. Reheat in a preheated 175ºC air fryer for 4 minutes, or until heated through.

## Sausage and Peppers

**Prep time: 7 minutes | Cook time: 35 minutes | Serves 4**

Oil, for spraying

900 g hot or sweet Italian-seasoned sausage links, cut into thick slices

4 large peppers of any color, seeded and cut into slices

1 onion, thinly sliced

1 tablespoon olive oil

1 tablespoon chopped fresh parsley

1 teaspoon dried oregano

1 teaspoon dried basil

1 teaspoon balsamic vinegar

1. Line the air fryer basket with parchment and spray lightly with oil. 2. In a large bowl, combine the sausage, peppers, and onion. 3. In a small bowl, whisk together the olive oil, parsley, oregano, basil, and balsamic vinegar. Pour the mixture over the sausage and peppers and toss until evenly coated. 4. Using a slotted spoon, transfer the mixture to the prepared basket, taking care to drain out as much excess liquid as possible. 5. Air fry at 175°C for 20 minutes, stir, and cook for another 15 minutes, or until the sausage is browned and the juices run clear.

## Blue Cheese Steak Salad

**Prep time: 30 minutes | Cook time: 22 minutes | Serves 4**

2 tablespoons balsamic vinegar

2 tablespoons red wine vinegar

1 tablespoon Dijon mustard

1 tablespoon granulated sweetener

1 teaspoon minced garlic

Sea salt and freshly ground black pepper, to taste

180 ml extra-virgin olive oil

450 g boneless rump steak

Avocado oil spray

1 small red onion, cut into ¼-inch-thick rounds

170 g baby spinach

120 ml cherry tomatoes, halved

85 g blue cheese, crumbled

1. In a blender, combine the balsamic vinegar, red wine vinegar, Dijon mustard, sweetener, and garlic. Season with salt and pepper and process until smooth. With the blender running, drizzle in the olive oil. Process until well combined. Transfer to a jar with a tight-fitting lid, and refrigerate until ready to serve (it will keep for up to 2 weeks). 2. Season the steak with salt and pepper and let sit at room temperature for at least 45 minutes, time permitting. 3. Set the air fryer to 200°C. Spray the steak with oil and place it in the air fryer basket. Air fry for 6 minutes. Flip the steak and spray it with more oil. Air fry for 6 minutes more for medium-rare or until the steak is done to your liking. 4. Transfer the steak to a plate, tent with a piece of aluminum foil, and allow it to rest. 5. Spray the onion slices with oil and place them in the air fryer basket. Cook at 200°C for 5 minutes. Flip the onion slices and spray them with more oil. Air fry for 5 minutes more. 6. Slice the steak diagonally into thin strips. Place the spinach, cherry tomatoes, onion slices, and steak in a large bowl. Toss with the desired amount of dressing. Sprinkle with crumbled blue cheese and serve.

## Mediterranean Beef Steaks

**Prep time: 20 minutes | Cook time: 20 minutes | Serves 4**

2 tablespoons soy sauce or tamari

3 heaping tablespoons fresh chives

2 tablespoons olive oil

3 tablespoons dry white wine

4 small-sized beef steaks

2 teaspoons smoked cayenne

pepper

½ teaspoon dried basil

½ teaspoon dried rosemary

1 teaspoon freshly ground black pepper

1 teaspoon sea salt, or more to taste

1. Firstly, coat the steaks with the cayenne pepper, black pepper, salt, basil, and rosemary. 2. Drizzle the steaks with olive oil, white wine, and soy sauce. 3. Finally, roast in the air fryer for 20 minutes at 170°C. Serve garnished with fresh chives. Bon appétit!

## Honey-Baked Pork Loin

**Prep time: 30 minutes | Cook time: 22 to 25 minutes | Serves 6**

60 ml honey

60 ml freshly squeezed lemon juice

2 tablespoons soy sauce

1 teaspoon garlic powder

1 (900 g) pork loin

2 tablespoons vegetable oil

1. In a medium bowl, whisk together the honey, lemon juice, soy sauce, and garlic powder. Reserve half of the mixture for basting during cooking. 2. Cut 5 slits in the pork loin and transfer it to a resealable bag. Add the remaining honey mixture. Seal the bag and refrigerate to marinate for at least 2 hours. 3. Preheat the air fryer to 200°C. Line the air fryer basket with parchment paper. 4. Remove the pork from the marinade, and place it on the parchment. Spritz with oil, then baste with the reserved marinade. 5. Cook for 15 minutes. Flip the pork, baste with more marinade and spritz with oil again. Cook for 7 to 10 minutes more until the internal temperature reaches 65°C. Let rest for 5 minutes before serving.

## Mongolian-Style Beef

**Prep time: 10 minutes | Cook time: 10 minutes | Serves 4**

| | |
|---|---|
| Oil, for spraying | 2 teaspoons toasted sesame oil |
| 60 ml cornflour | 1 tablespoon minced garlic |
| 450 g bavette or skirt steak, thinly sliced | ½ teaspoon ground ginger |
| 180 ml packed light brown sugar | 120 ml water |
| 120 ml soy sauce | Cooked white rice or ramen noodles, for serving |

1. Line the air fryer basket with parchment and spray lightly with oil. 2. Place the cornflour in a bowl and dredge the steak until evenly coated. Shake off any excess cornflour. 3. Place the steak in the prepared basket and spray lightly with oil. 4. Roast at 200ºC for 5 minutes, flip, and cook for another 5 minutes. 5. In a small saucepan, combine the brown sugar, soy sauce, sesame oil, garlic, ginger, and water and bring to a boil over medium-high heat, stirring frequently. Remove from the heat. 6. Transfer the meat to the sauce and toss until evenly coated. Let sit for about 5 minutes so the steak absorbs the flavors. Serve with white rice or ramen noodles.

## Pork Schnitzel with Dill Sauce

**Prep time: 5 minutes | Cook time: 24 minutes | Serves 4 to 6**

| | |
|---|---|
| 6 bonelesspork chops (about 680 g) | 3 tablespoons butter, melted |
| 120 ml flour | 2 tablespoons vegetable or olive oil |
| 1½ teaspoons salt | lemon wedges |
| Freshly ground black pepper, to taste | Dill Sauce: |
| 2 eggs | 235 ml chicken stock |
| 120 ml milk | 1½ tablespoons cornflour |
| 355 ml toasted fine bread crumbs | 80 ml sour cream |
| 1 teaspoon paprika | 1½ tablespoons chopped fresh dill |
| | Salt and pepper, to taste |

1. Trim the excess fat from the pork chops and pound each chop with a meat mallet between two pieces of plastic wrap until they are ½-inch thick. 2. Set up a dredging station. Combine the flour, salt, and black pepper in a shallow dish. Whisk the eggs and milk together in a second shallow dish. Finally, combine the bread crumbs and paprika in a third shallow dish. 3. Dip each flattened pork chop in the flour. Shake off the excess flour and dip each chop into the egg mixture. Finally dip them into the bread crumbs and press the bread crumbs onto the meat firmly. Place each finished chop on a baking sheet until they are all coated. 4. Preheat the air fryer to 200ºC. 5. Combine the melted butter and the oil in a small bowl and lightly brush both sides of the coated pork chops. Do not brush the chops too heavily or the breading will not be as crispy. 6. Air fry one schnitzel at a time for 4 minutes, turning it over halfway through the cooking time. Hold the cooked schnitzels warm on a baking pan in a 75ºC oven while you finish air frying the rest. 7. While the schnitzels are cooking, whisk the chicken stock and cornflour together in a small saucepan over medium-high heat on the stovetop. Bring the mixture to a boil and simmer for 2 minutes. Remove the saucepan from heat and whisk in the sour cream. Add the chopped fresh dill and season with salt and pepper. 8. Transfer the pork schnitzel to a platter and serve with dill sauce and lemon wedges.

## Sichuan Cumin Lamb

**Prep time: 30 minutes | Cook time: 10 minutes | Serves 4**

| | |
|---|---|
| Lamb: | 1 tablespoon light soy sauce |
| 2 tablespoons cumin seeds | 1 tablespoon minced garlic |
| 1 teaspoon Sichuan peppercorns, or ½ teaspoon cayenne pepper | 2 fresh red chiles, chopped |
| | 1 teaspoon coarse or flaky salt |
| 450 g lamb (preferably shoulder), cut into ½ by 2-inch pieces | ¼ teaspoon sugar |
| | For Serving: |
| | 2 spring onions, chopped |
| 2 tablespoons vegetable oil | Large handful of chopped fresh coriander |

1. For the lamb: In a dry skillet, toast the cumin seeds and Sichuan peppercorns (if using) over medium heat, stirring frequently, until fragrant, 1 to 2 minutes. Remove from the heat and let cool. Use a mortar and pestle to coarsely grind the toasted spices. 2. Use a fork to pierce the lamb pieces to allow the marinade to penetrate better. In a large bowl or resealable plastic bag, combine the toasted spices, vegetable oil, soy sauce, garlic, chiles, salt, and sugar. Add the lamb to the bag. Seal and massage to coat. Marinate at room temperature for 30 minutes. 3. Place the lamb in a single layer in the air fryer basket. Set the air fryer to 175ºC for 10 minutes. Use a meat thermometer to ensure the lamb has reached an internal temperature of 65ºC (medium-rare). 4. Transfer the lamb to a serving bowl. Stir in the spring onionspring onions and coriander and serve.

## Greek Lamb Pitta Pockets

**Prep time: 15 minutes | Cook time: 6 minutes | Serves 4**

Dressing:

235 ml plain yogurt

1 tablespoon lemon juice

1 teaspoon dried dill, crushed

1 teaspoon ground oregano

½ teaspoon salt

Meatballs:

230 g lamb mince

1 tablespoon diced onion

1 teaspoon dried parsley

1 teaspoon dried dill, crushed

¼ teaspoon oregano

¼ teaspoon coriander

¼ teaspoon ground cumin

¼ teaspoon salt

4 pitta halves

Suggested Toppings:

1 red onion, slivered

1 medium cucumber, deseeded, thinly sliced

Crumbled feta cheese

Sliced black olives

Chopped fresh peppers

1. Preheat the air fryer to 200ºC. 2. Stir the dressing ingredients together in a small bowl and refrigerate while preparing lamb. 3. Combine all meatball ingredients in a large bowl and stir to distribute seasonings. 4. Shape meat mixture into 12 small meatballs, rounded or slightly flattened if you prefer. 5. Transfer the meatballs in the preheated air fryer and air fry for 6 minutes, until well done. Remove and drain on paper towels. 6. To serve, pile meatballs and the choice of toppings in pitta pockets and drizzle with dressing.

## Rosemary Roast Beef

**Prep time: 30 minutes | Cook time: 30 to 35 minutes | Serves 8**

1 (900 g) beef roasting joint, tied with kitchen string

Sea salt and freshly ground black pepper, to taste

2 teaspoons minced garlic

2 tablespoons finely chopped fresh rosemary

60 ml avocado oil

1. Season the roast generously with salt and pepper. 2. In a small bowl, whisk together the garlic, rosemary, and avocado oil. Rub this all over the roast. Cover loosely with aluminum foil or plastic wrap and refrigerate for at least 12 hours or up to 2 days. 3. Remove the roast from the refrigerator and allow to sit at room temperature for about 1 hour. 4. Set the air fryer to 165ºC. Place the roast in the air fryer basket and roast for 15 minutes. Flip the roast and cook for 15 to 20 minutes more, until the meat is browned and an instant-read thermometer reads 50ºC at the thickest part (for medium-rare). 5. Transfer the meat to a cutting board, and let it rest for 15 minutes before thinly slicing and serving.

## London Broil with Herb Butter

**Prep time: 30 minutes | Cook time: 20 to 25 minutes | Serves 4**

680 g bavette or skirt steak

60 ml olive oil

2 tablespoons balsamic vinegar

1 tablespoon Worcestershire sauce

4 cloves garlic, minced

Herb Butter:

6 tablespoons unsalted butter,

softened

1 tablespoon chopped fresh parsley

¼ teaspoon salt

¼ teaspoon dried ground rosemary or thyme

¼ teaspoon garlic powder

Pinch of red pepper flakes

1. Place the beef in a gallon-size resealable bag. In a small bowl, whisk together the olive oil, balsamic vinegar, Worcestershire sauce, and garlic. Pour the marinade over the beef, massaging gently to coat, and seal the bag. Let sit at room temperature for an hour or refrigerate overnight. 2. To make the herb butter: In a small bowl, mix the butter with the parsley, salt, rosemary, garlic powder, and red pepper flakes until smooth. Cover and refrigerate until ready to use. 3. Preheat the air fryer to 200ºC. 4. Remove the beef from the marinade (discard the marinade) and place the beef in the air fryer basket. Pausing halfway through the cooking time to turn the meat, air fry for 20 to 25 minutes, until a thermometer inserted into the thickest part indicates the desired doneness, 50ºC (rare) to 65ºC (medium). Let the beef rest for 10 minutes before slicing. Serve topped with the herb butter.

## Bone-in Pork Chops

**Prep time: 5 minutes | Cook time: 10 to 12 minutes | Serves 2**

450 g bone-in pork chops

1 tablespoon avocado oil

1 teaspoon smoked paprika

½ teaspoon onion granules

¼ teaspoon cayenne pepper

Sea salt and freshly ground black pepper, to taste

1. Brush the pork chops with the avocado oil. In a small dish, mix together the smoked paprika, onion granules, cayenne pepper, and salt and black pepper to taste. Sprinkle the seasonings over both sides of the pork chops. 2. Set the air fryer to 200ºC. Place the chops in the air fryer basket in a single layer, working in batches if necessary. Air fry for 10 to 12 minutes, until an instant-read thermometer reads 65ºC at the chops' thickest point. 3. Remove the chops from the air fryer and allow them to rest for 5 minutes before serving.

## Panko Pork Chops

**Prep time: 10 minutes | Cook time: 12 minutes | Serves 4**

| | |
|---|---|
| 4 boneless pork chops, excess fat trimmed | 1½ teaspoons paprika |
| ¼ teaspoon salt | ½ teaspoon granulated garlic |
| 2 eggs | ½ teaspoon onion granules |
| 355 ml panko bread crumbs | 1 teaspoon chili powder |
| 3 tablespoons grated Parmesan cheese | ¼ teaspoon freshly ground black pepper |
| | Olive oil spray |

1. Sprinkle the pork chops with salt on both sides and let them sit while you prepare the seasonings and egg wash. 2. In a shallow medium bowl, beat the eggs. 3. In another shallow medium bowl, stir together the panko, Parmesan cheese, paprika, granulated garlic, onion granules, chili powder, and pepper. 4. Dip the pork chops in the egg and in the panko mixture to coat. Firmly press the crumbs onto the chops. 5. Insert the crisper plate into the basket and the basket into the unit. Preheat the unit by selecting AIR ROAST, setting the temperature to 200ºC, and setting the time to 3 minutes. Select START/STOP to begin. 6. Once the unit is preheated, spray the crisper plate with olive oil. Place the pork chops into the basket and spray them with olive oil. 7. Select AIR ROAST, set the temperature to 200ºC, and set the time to 12 minutes. Select START/STOP to begin. 8. After 6 minutes, flip the pork chops and spray them with more olive oil. Resume cooking. 9. When the cooking is complete, the chops should be golden and crispy and a food thermometer should register 65ºC. Serve immediately.

## Homemade Beefy Poppers

**Prep time: 15 minutes | Cook time: 15 minutes | Makes 8 poppers**

| | |
|---|---|
| 8 medium jalapeño peppers, stemmed, halved, and seeded | 1 teaspoon fine sea salt |
| 1 (230 g) package cream cheese (or cream cheese style spread for dairy-free), softened | ½ teaspoon ground black pepper |
| 900 g beef mince (85% lean) | 8 slices thin-cut bacon |
| | Fresh coriander leaves, for garnish |

1. Spray the air fryer basket with avocado oil. Preheat the air fryer to 200ºC. 2. Stuff each jalapeño half with a few tablespoons of cream cheese. Place the halves back together again to form 8 jalapeños. 3. Season the beef mince with the salt and pepper and mix with your hands to incorporate. Flatten about 110 g of beef in the palm of your hand and place a stuffed jalapeño in the center.

Fold the beef around the jalapeño, forming an egg shape. Wrap the beef-covered jalapeño with a slice of bacon and secure it with a toothpick. 4. Place the jalapeños in the air fryer basket, leaving space between them (if you're using a smaller air fryer, work in batches if necessary), and air fry for 15 minutes, or until the beef is cooked through and the bacon is crispy. Garnish with coriander before serving. 5. Store leftovers in an airtight container in the fridge for 3 days or in the freezer for up to a month. Reheat in a preheated 175ºC air fryer for 4 minutes, or until heated through and the bacon is crispy.

## Sausage and Cauliflower Arancini

**Prep time: 30 minutes | Cook time: 28 to 32 minutes | Serves 6**

| | |
|---|---|
| Avocado oil spray | 85 g cream cheese |
| 170 g Italian-seasoned sausage, casings removed | 110 g Cheddar cheese, shredded |
| 60 ml diced onion | 1 large egg |
| 1 teaspoon minced garlic | 120 ml finely ground blanched almond flour |
| 1 teaspoon dried thyme | 60 ml finely grated Parmesan cheese |
| Sea salt and freshly ground black pepper, to taste | Keto-friendly marinara sauce, for serving |
| 120 ml cauliflower rice | |

1. Spray a large skillet with oil and place it over medium-high heat. Once the skillet is hot, put the sausage in the skillet and cook for 7 minutes, breaking up the meat with the back of a spoon. 2. Reduce the heat to medium and add the onion. Cook for 5 minutes, then add the garlic, thyme, and salt and pepper to taste. Cook for 1 minute more. 3. Add the cauliflower rice and cream cheese to the skillet. Cook for 7 minutes, stirring frequently, until the cream cheese melts and the cauliflower is tender. 4. Remove the skillet from the heat and stir in the Cheddar cheese. Using a cookie scoop, form the mixture into 1½-inch balls. Place the balls on a parchment paper-lined baking sheet. Freeze for 30 minutes. 5. Place the egg in a shallow bowl and beat it with a fork. In a separate bowl, stir together the almond flour and Parmesan cheese. 6. Dip the cauliflower balls into the egg, then coat them with the almond flour mixture, gently pressing the mixture to the balls to adhere. 7. Set the air fryer to 200ºC. Spray the cauliflower rice balls with oil, and arrange them in a single layer in the air fryer basket, working in batches if necessary. Air fry for 5 minutes. Flip the rice balls and spray them with more oil. Air fry for 3 to 7 minutes longer, until the balls are golden brown. 8. Serve warm with marinara sauce.

## Greek Pork with Tzatziki Sauce

**Prep time: 30 minutes | Cook time: 50 minutes | Serves 4**

Greek Pork:

900 g pork loin roasting joint

Salt and black pepper, to taste

1 teaspoon smoked paprika

½ teaspoon mustard seeds

½ teaspoon celery salt

1 teaspoon fennel seeds

1 teaspoon chili powder

1 teaspoon turmeric powder

½ teaspoon ground ginger

2 tablespoons olive oil

2 cloves garlic, finely chopped

Tzatziki:

½ cucumber, finely chopped and squeezed

235 ml full-fat Greek yogurt

1 garlic clove, minced

1 tablespoon extra-virgin olive oil

1 teaspoon balsamic vinegar

1 teaspoon minced fresh dill

A pinch of salt

1. Toss all ingredients for Greek pork in a large mixing bowl. Toss until the meat is well coated. 2. Cook in the preheated air fryer at 180ºC for 30 minutes; turn over and cook another 20 minutes. 3. Meanwhile, prepare the tzatziki by mixing all the tzatziki ingredients. Place in your refrigerator until ready to use. 4. Serve the pork sirloin roast with the chilled tzatziki on the side. Enjoy!

## Onion Pork Kebabs

**Prep time: 22 minutes | Cook time: 18 minutes | Serves 3**

2 tablespoons tomato purée

½ fresh green chilli, minced

⅓ teaspoon paprika

450 g pork mince

120 ml spring onions, finely chopped

3 cloves garlic, peeled and finely minced

1 teaspoon ground black pepper, or more to taste

1 teaspoon salt, or more to taste

1. Thoroughly combine all ingredients in a mixing dish. Then form your mixture into sausage shapes. 2. Cook for 18 minutes at 180ºC. Mound salad on a serving platter, top with air-fried kebabs and serve warm. Bon appétit!

# Chapter 7 Desserts

# Chapter 7 Desserts

## Cream Cheese Shortbread Cookies

**Prep time: 30 minutes | Cook time: 20 minutes |**
**Makes 12 cookies**

60 ml coconut oil, melted

55 g cream cheese, softened

100 g granulated sweetener

1 large egg, whisked

190 g blanched finely ground almond flour

1 teaspoon almond extract

1. Combine all ingredients in a large bowl to form a firm ball. 2. Place dough on a sheet of plastic wrap and roll into a 12-inch-long log shape. Roll log in plastic wrap and place in refrigerator 30 minutes to chill. 3. Remove log from plastic and slice into twelve equal cookies. Cut two sheets of baking paper to fit air fryer basket. Place six cookies on each ungreased sheet. Place one sheet with cookies into air fryer basket. Adjust the temperature to 160ºC and bake for 10 minutes, turning cookies halfway through cooking. They will be lightly golden when done. Repeat with remaining cookies. 4. Let cool 15 minutes before serving to avoid crumbling.

## Blackberry Peach Cobbler with Vanilla

**Prep time: 10 minutes | Cook time: 20 minutes | Serves 4**

Filling:

170 g blackberries

250 g chopped peaches, cut into ½-inch thick slices

2 teaspoons arrowroot or cornflour

2 tablespoons coconut sugar

1 teaspoon lemon juice

Topping:

2 tablespoons sunflower oil

1 tablespoon maple syrup

1 teaspoon vanilla

3 tablespoons coconut sugar

40 g rolled oats

45 g whole-wheat pastry, or plain flour

1 teaspoon cinnamon

¼ teaspoon nutmeg

⅛ teaspoon sea salt

Make the Filling: 1. Combine the blackberries, peaches, arrowroot, coconut sugar, and lemon juice in a baking pan. 2. Using a rubber spatula, stir until well incorporated. Set aside. Make the Topping: 3. Preheat the air fryer to 160ºC 4. Combine the oil, maple syrup, and vanilla in a mixing bowl and stir well. Whisk in the remaining ingredients. Spread this mixture evenly over the filling. 5. Place the pan in the air fryer basket and bake for 20 minutes, or until the topping is crispy and golden brown. Serve warm

## Sweet Potato Donut Holes

**Prep time: 10 minutes | Cook time: 4 to 5 minutes**
**per batch | Makes 18 donut holes**

125 g plain flour

65 g granulated sugar

¼ teaspoon baking soda

1 teaspoon baking powder

⅛ teaspoon salt

125 g cooked & mashed purple

sweet potatoes

1 egg, beaten

2 tablespoons butter, melted

1 teaspoon pure vanilla extract

Coconut, or avocado oil for misting or cooking spray

1. Preheat the air fryer to 200ºC. 2. In a large bowl, stir together the flour, sugar, baking soda, baking powder, and salt. 3. In a separate bowl, combine the potatoes, egg, butter, and vanilla and mix well. 4. Add potato mixture to dry ingredients and stir into a soft dough. 5. Shape dough into 1½-inch balls. Mist lightly with oil or cooking spray. 6. Place 9 donut holes in air fryer basket, leaving a little space in between. Cook for 4 to 5 minutes, until done in center and lightly browned outside. 7. Repeat step 6 to cook remaining donut holes.

## Coconut Macaroons

**Prep time: 5 minutes | Cook time: 8 to 10 minutes |**
**Makes 12 macaroons**

120 g desiccated, sweetened coconut

4½ teaspoons plain flour

2 tablespoons sugar

1 egg white

½ teaspoon almond extract

1. Preheat the air fryer to 165ºC. 2. In a medium bowl, mix all ingredients together. 3. Shape coconut mixture into 12 balls. 4. Place all 12 macaroons in air fryer basket. They won't expand, so you can place them close together, but they shouldn't touch. 5. Air fry for 8 to 10 minutes, until golden.

## Vanilla Scones

**Prep time: 20 minutes | Cook time: 10 minutes | Serves 6**

110 g coconut flour

½ teaspoon baking powder

1 teaspoon apple cider vinegar

2 teaspoons mascarpone

60 ml heavy cream

1 teaspoon vanilla extract

1 tablespoon granulated sweetener

Cooking spray

1. In the mixing bowl, mix coconut flour with baking powder, apple cider vinegar, mascarpone, heavy cream, vanilla extract, and sweetener. 2. Knead the dough and cut into scones. 3. Then put them in the air fryer basket and sprinkle with cooking spray. 4. Cook the vanilla scones at 185ºC for 10 minutes.

## Apple Wedges with Apricots

**Prep time: 5 minutes | Cook time: 15 to 18 minutes | Serves 4**

4 large apples, peeled and sliced into 8 wedges

2 tablespoons light olive oil

95 g dried apricots, chopped

1 to 2 tablespoons granulated sugar

½ teaspoon ground cinnamon

1. Preheat the air fryer to 180ºC. 2. Toss the apple wedges with the olive oil in a mixing bowl until well coated. 3. Place the apple wedges in the air fryer basket and air fry for 12 to 15 minutes. 4. Sprinkle with the dried apricots and air fry for another 3 minutes. 5. Meanwhile, thoroughly combine the sugar and cinnamon in a small bowl. 6. Remove the apple wedges from the basket to a plate. Serve sprinkled with the sugar mixture.

## Homemade Cherry Pie

**Prep time: 15 minutes | Cook time: 35 minutes | Serves 6**

Plain flour, for dusting

1 package of shortcrust pastry, cut in half, at room temperature

350 g can cherry pie filling

1 egg

1 tablespoon water

1 tablespoon sugar

1. Dust a work surface with flour and place the piecrust on it. Roll out the piecrust. Invert a shallow air fryer baking pan, or your own pie pan that fits inside the air fryer basket, on top of the dough. Trim the dough around the pan, making your cut ½ inch wider than the pan itself. 2. Repeat with the second piecrust but make the cut the same size as or slightly smaller than the pan. 3. Put the larger crust in the bottom of the baking pan. Don't stretch the dough. Gently press it into the pan. 4. Spoon in enough cherry pie filling to fill the crust. Do not overfill. 5. Using a knife or pizza cutter, cut the second piecrust into 1-inch-wide strips. Weave the strips in a lattice pattern over the top of the cherry pie filling. 6. Insert the crisper plate into the basket and the basket into the unit. Preheat to 165ºC. 7. In a small bowl, whisk the egg and water. Gently brush the egg wash over the top of the pie. Sprinkle with the sugar and cover the pie with aluminum foil. 8. Once the unit is preheated, place the pie into the basket. 9. Bake for 30 minutes, remove the foil and resume cooking for 3 to 5 minutes more. The finished pie should have a flaky golden-brown crust and bubbling pie filling. 10. When the cooking is complete, serve warm. Refrigerate leftovers for a few days.

## Homemade S'mores

**Prep time: 5 minutes | Cook time: 30 seconds | Makes 8 s'mores**

Coconut, or avocado oil, for spraying

8 digestive biscuits

2 (45 g) chocolate bars

4 large marshmallows

1. Line the air fryer basket with baking paper and spray lightly with oil. 2. Place 4 biscuits into the prepared basket. 3. Break the chocolate bars in half, and place 1/2 on top of each biscuit. Top with 1 marshmallow. 4. Air fry at 190ºC for 30 seconds, or until the marshmallows are puffed, golden brown and slightly melted. 5. Top with the remaining biscuits and serve.

## Pecan and Cherry Stuffed Apples

**Prep time: 10 minutes | Cook time: 20 minutes | Serves 4**

4 apples (about 565 g)

40 g chopped pecans

50 g dried tart cherries

1 tablespoon melted butter

3 tablespoons brown sugar

¼ teaspoon allspice

Pinch salt

Ice cream, for serving

1. Cut off top ½ inch from each apple; reserve tops. With a melon baller, core through stem ends without breaking through the bottom. (Do not trim bases.) 2. Preheat the air fryer to 175ºC. Combine pecans, cherries, butter, brown sugar, allspice, and a pinch of salt. Stuff mixture into the hollow centers of the apples. Cover with apple tops. Put in the air fryer basket, using tongs. Air fry for 20 to 25 minutes, or just until tender. 3. Serve warm with ice cream.

## Strawberry Shortcake

**Prep time: 10 minutes | Cook time: 25 minutes | Serves 6**

| | |
|---|---|
| 2 tablespoons coconut oil | 1 teaspoon baking powder |
| 110 g blanched finely ground almond flour | 1 teaspoon vanilla extract |
| 2 large eggs, whisked | 240 g heavy cream, whipped |
| 100 g granulated sweetener | 6 medium fresh strawberries, hulled and sliced |

1. In a large bowl, combine coconut oil, flour, eggs, sweetener, baking powder, and vanilla. Pour batter into an ungreased round nonstick baking dish. 2. Place dish into air fryer basket. Adjust the temperature to 150°C and bake for 25 minutes. When done, shortcake should be golden, and a toothpick inserted in the middle will come out clean. 3. Remove dish from fryer and let cool 1 hour. 4. Once cooled, top cake with whipped cream and strawberries to serve.

## Lemon Curd Pavlova

**Prep time: 10 minutes | Cook time: 1 hour | Serves 4**

| | |
|---|---|
| Shell: | 100 g powdered sweetener |
| 3 large egg whites | 120 ml lemon juice |
| ¼ teaspoon cream of tartar | 4 large eggs |
| 75 g powdered sweetener | 120 ml coconut oil |
| 1 teaspoon grated lemon zest | For Garnish (Optional): |
| 1 teaspoon lemon extract | Blueberries |
| Lemon Curd: | powdered sweetener |

1. Preheat the air fryer to 135°C. Thoroughly grease a pie pan with butter or coconut oil. 2. Make the shell: In a small bowl, use a hand mixer to beat the egg whites and cream of tartar until soft peaks form. With the mixer on low, slowly sprinkle in the sweetener and mix until it's completely incorporated. 3. Add the lemon zest and lemon extract and continue to beat with the hand mixer until stiff peaks form. 4. Spoon the mixture into the greased pie pan, then smooth it across the bottom, up the sides, and onto the rim to form a shell. Bake for 1 hour, then turn off the air fryer and let the shell stand in the air fryer for 20 minutes. (The shell can be made up to 3 days ahead and stored in an airtight container in the refrigerator, if desired.) 5. While the shell bakes, make the lemon curd: In a medium-sized heavy-bottomed saucepan, whisk together the sweetener, lemon juice, and eggs. Add the coconut oil and place the pan on the stovetop over medium heat. Once the oil is melted, whisk constantly until the mixture thickens and thickly coats the back of a spoon, about 10 minutes. Do not allow the mixture to come to a boil. 6. Pour the lemon curd mixture through a fine-mesh strainer into a medium-sized bowl. Place the bowl inside a larger bowl filled with ice water and whisk occasionally until the curd is completely cool, about 15 minutes. 7. Place the lemon curd on top of the shell and garnish with blueberries and powdered sweetener, if desired. Store leftovers in the refrigerator for up to 4 days.

## Almond-Roasted Pears

**Prep time: 10 minutes | Cook time: 15 to 20 minutes | Serves 4**

| | |
|---|---|
| Yogurt Topping: | 2 whole pears |
| 140-170 g pot vanilla Greek yogurt | 4 crushed Biscoff biscuits |
| ¼ teaspoon almond flavoring | 1 tablespoon flaked almonds |
| | 1 tablespoon unsalted butter |

1. Stir the almond flavoring into yogurt and set aside while preparing pears. 2. Halve each pear and spoon out the core. 3. Place pear halves in air fryer basket, skin side down. 4. Stir together the crushed biscuits and almonds. Place a quarter of this mixture into the hollow of each pear half. 5. Cut butter into 4 pieces and place one piece on top of biscuit mixture in each pear. 6. Roast at 185°C for 15 to 20 minutes, or until pears have cooked through but are still slightly firm. 7. Serve pears warm with a dollop of yogurt topping.

## Roasted Honey Pears

**Prep time: 7 minutes | Cook time: 18 to 23 minutes | Serves 4**

| | |
|---|---|
| 2 large Bosc pears, halved lengthwise and seeded | ½ teaspoon ground cinnamon |
| 3 tablespoons honey | 30 g walnuts, chopped |
| 1 tablespoon unsalted butter | 55 g part-skim ricotta cheese, divided |

1. Insert the crisper plate into the basket and the basket into the unit. Preheat to 175°C. 2. In a 6-by-2-inch round pan, place the pears cut-side up. 3. In a small microwave-safe bowl, melt the honey, butter, and cinnamon. Brush this mixture over the cut sides of the pears. Pour 3 tablespoons of water around the pears in the pan. 4. Once the unit is preheated, place the pan into the basket. 5. After about 18 minutes, check the pears. They should be tender when pierced with a fork and slightly crisp on the edges. If not, resume cooking. 6. When the cooking is complete, baste the pears once with the liquid in the pan. Carefully remove the pears from the pan and place on a serving plate. Drizzle each with some liquid from the pan, sprinkle the walnuts on top, and serve with a spoonful of ricotta cheese.

## Luscious Coconut Pie

**Prep time: 5 minutes | Cook time: 45 minutes | Serves 6**

100 g desiccated, unsweetened coconut, plus 25 g, divided

2 eggs

355 ml almond milk

100 g granulated sweetener

55 g coconut flour

55 g unsalted butter, melted

1½ teaspoons vanilla extract

¼ teaspoon salt

2 tablespoons powdered sweetener (optional)

120 g whipping cream, whipped until stiff (optional)

1. Spread 25 g of the coconut in the bottom of a pie plate and place in the air fryer basket. Set the air fryer to 175ºC and air fry the coconut while the air fryer preheats, about 5 minutes, until golden brown. Transfer the coconut to a small bowl and set aside for garnish. Brush the pie plate with oil and set aside. 2. In a large bowl, combine the remaining 100 g shredded coconut, eggs, milk, granulated sweetener, coconut flour, butter, vanilla, and salt. Whisk until smooth. Pour the batter into the prepared pie plate and air fry for 40 to 45 minutes, or until a toothpick inserted into the center of the pie comes out clean. (Check halfway through the baking time and rotate the pan, if necessary, for even baking.) 3. Remove the pie from the air fryer and place on a baking rack to cool completely. Garnish with the reserved toasted coconut and the powdered sweetener or whipped cream, if desired. Cover and refrigerate leftover pie for up to 3 days.

## Tortilla Fried Hand Pies

**Prep time: 10 minutes | Cook time: 5 minutes per batch | Makes 12 pies**

12 small flour tortillas (4-inch diameter)

160 g fig jam

20 g slivered almonds

2 tablespoons desiccated, unsweetened coconut

Coconut, or avocado oil for misting or cooking spray

1. Wrap refrigerated tortillas in damp paper towels and heat in microwave 30 seconds to warm. 2. Working with one tortilla at a time, place 2 teaspoons fig jam, 1 teaspoon slivered almonds, and ½ teaspoon coconut in the center of each. 3. Moisten outer edges of tortilla all around. 4. Fold one side of tortilla over filling, to make a half-moon shape, and press down lightly on center. Using the tines of a fork, press down firmly on edges of tortilla to seal in filling. 5. Mist both sides with oil or cooking spray. 6. Place hand pies in air fryer basket, close, but not overlapping. It's fine to lean some against the sides and corners of the basket. You may need to cook in 2 batches. 7. Air fry at 200ºC for 5 minutes, or until lightly browned. Serve hot. 8. Refrigerate any leftover pies in a closed container. To serve later, toss them back in the air fryer basket and cook for 2 to 3 minutes to reheat.

## Orange Gooey Butter Cake

**Prep time: 5 minutes | Cook time: 1 hour 25 minutes | Serves 6 to 8**

Crust Layer:

60 g plain flour

50 g granulated sugar

½ teaspoon baking powder

⅛ teaspoon salt

60 g unsalted butter, melted

1 egg

1 teaspoon orange extract

2 tablespoons orange zest

Gooey Butter Layer:

230 g cream cheese, softened

110 g unsalted butter, melted

2 eggs

2 teaspoons orange extract

2 tablespoons orange zest

480 g icing sugar

Garnish:

Icing sugar

Orange slices

1. Preheat the air fryer to 175ºC. 2. Grease a cake pan and line the bottom with baking paper. Combine the flour, sugar, baking powder and salt in a bowl. Add the melted butter, egg, orange extract and orange zest. Mix well and press this mixture into the bottom of the greased cake pan. Lower the pan into the basket using an aluminum foil sling (fold a piece of aluminum foil into a strip about 2-inches wide by 24-inches long). Fold the ends of the aluminum foil over the top of the dish before returning the basket to the air fryer. Air fry uncovered for 8 minutes. 3. Make the gooey butter layer: Beat the cream cheese, melted butter, eggs, orange extract and orange zest in a large bowl using an electric hand mixer. Add the icing sugar in stages, beat until smooth with each addition. Pour this mixture on top of the baked crust in the cake pan. Wrap the pan with a piece of greased aluminum foil, tenting the top of the foil to leave a little room for the cake to rise. 4. Air fry for 60 minutes. Remove the aluminum foil and air fry for an additional 17 minutes. 5. Let the cake cool inside the pan for at least 10 minutes. Then, run a butter knife around the cake and let the cake cool completely in the pan. When cooled, run the butter knife around the edges of the cake again and invert it onto a plate and then back onto a serving platter. Sprinkle the icing sugar over the top of the cake and garnish with orange slices.

## Pecan Butter Cookies

**Prep time: 5 minutes | Cook time: 24 minutes |**
**Makes 12 cookies**

125 g chopped pecans

110 g salted butter, melted

55 g coconut flour

150 g granulated sweetener, divided

1 teaspoon vanilla extract

1. In a food processor, blend together pecans, butter, flour, 100 g sweetener, and vanilla 1 minute until a dough forms. 2. Form dough into twelve individual cookie balls, about 1 tablespoon each. 3. Cut three pieces of baking paper to fit air fryer basket. Place four cookies on each ungreased baking paper and place one piece baking paper with cookies into air fryer basket. Adjust air fryer temperature to 165°C and set the timer for 8 minutes. Repeat cooking with remaining batches. 4. When the timer goes off, allow cookies to cool 5 minutes on a large serving plate until cool enough to handle. While still warm, dust cookies with remaining granulated sweetener. Allow to cool completely, about 15 minutes, before serving.

## Air Fryer Apple Fritters

**Prep time: 30 minutes | Cook time: 7 to 8 minutes |**
**Serves 6**

1 chopped, peeled Granny Smith apple

115 g granulated sugar

1 teaspoon ground cinnamon

120 g plain flour

1 teaspoon baking powder

1 teaspoon salt

2 tablespoons milk

2 tablespoons butter, melted

1 large egg, beaten

Cooking spray

25 g icing sugar (optional)

1. Mix together the apple, granulated sugar, and cinnamon in a small bowl. Allow to sit for 30 minutes. 2. Combine the flour, baking powder, and salt in a medium bowl. Add the milk, butter, and egg and stir to incorporate. 3. Pour the apple mixture into the bowl of flour mixture and stir with a spatula until a dough forms. 4. Make the fritters: On a clean work surface, divide the dough into 12 equal portions and shape into 1-inch balls. Flatten them into patties with your hands. 5. Preheat the air fryer to 175°C. Line the air fryer basket with baking paper and spray it with cooking spray. 6. Transfer the apple fritters onto the baking paper, evenly spaced but not too close together. Spray the fritters with cooking spray. 7. Bake for 7 to 8 minutes until lightly browned. Flip the fritters halfway through the cooking time. 8. Remove from the basket to a plate and serve with the confectioners' sugar sprinkled on top, if desired.

## Chocolate Croissants

**Prep time: 5 minutes | Cook time: 24 minutes | Serves 8**

1 sheet frozen puff pastry, thawed

100 g chocolate-hazelnut spread

1 large egg, beaten

1. On a lightly floured surface, roll puff pastry into a 14-inch square. Cut pastry into quarters to form 4 squares. Cut each square diagonally to form 8 triangles. 2. Spread 2 teaspoons chocolate-hazelnut spread on each triangle; from wider end, roll up pastry. Brush egg on top of each roll. 3. Preheat the air fryer to 190°C. Air fry rolls in batches, 3 or 4 at a time, 8 minutes per batch, or until pastry is golden brown. 4. Cool on a wire rack; serve while warm or at room temperature.

## Chocolate Soufflés

**Prep time: 5 minutes | Cook time: 14 minutes | Serves 2**

Butter and sugar for greasing the ramekins

85 g semi-sweet chocolate, chopped

55 g unsalted butter

2 eggs, yolks and white separated

3 tablespoons granulated sugar

½ teaspoon pure vanilla extract

2 tablespoons plain flour

Icing sugar, for dusting the finished soufflés

Heavy cream, for serving

1. Butter and sugar two 6-ounce (170 g) ramekins. (Butter the ramekins and then coat the butter with sugar by shaking it around in the ramekin and dumping out any excess.) 2. Melt the chocolate and butter together, either in the microwave or in a double boiler. In a separate bowl, beat the egg yolks vigorously. Add the sugar and the vanilla extract and beat well again. Drizzle in the chocolate and butter, mixing well. Stir in the flour, combining until there are no lumps. 3. Preheat the air fryer to 165°C. 4. In a separate bowl, whisk the egg whites to soft peak stage (the point at which the whites can almost stand up on the end of your whisk). Fold the whipped egg whites into the chocolate mixture gently and in stages. 5. Transfer the batter carefully to the buttered ramekins, leaving about ½-inch at the top. (You may have a little extra batter, depending on how airy the batter is, so you might be able to squeeze out a third soufflé if you want to.) Place the ramekins into the air fryer basket and air fry for 14 minutes. The soufflés should have risen nicely and be brown on top. (Don't worry if the top gets a little dark, you'll be covering it with icing sugar in the next step.) 6. Dust with icing sugar and serve immediately with heavy cream to pour over the top at the table.

## Baked Apple with Pecans

**Prep time: 10 minutes | Cook time: 20 minutes |**
**Makes 6 apple halves**

| | |
|---|---|
| 3 small Pink Lady or other baking apples | 3 tablespoons chopped pecans |
| 3 tablespoons maple syrup | 1 tablespoon firm butter, cut into 6 pieces |

1. Put 6.5 tablespoons water in the drawer of the air fryer. 2. Wash apples well and dry them. 3. Split apples in half. Remove core and a little of the flesh to make a cavity for the pecans. 4. Place apple halves in air fryer basket, cut side up. 5. Spoon 1½ teaspoons pecans into each cavity. 6. Spoon ½ tablespoon maple syrup over pecans in each apple. 7. Top each apple with 1 piece of butter. 8. Bake at 185ºC for 20 minutes, until apples are tender.

## Gingerbread

**Prep time: 5 minutes | Cook time: 20 minutes |**
**Makes 1 loaf**

| | |
|---|---|
| Cooking spray | ⅛ teaspoon salt |
| 125 g plain flour | 1 egg |
| 2 tablespoons granulated sugar | 70 g treacle |
| ¾ teaspoon ground ginger | 120 ml buttermilk |
| ¼ teaspoon cinnamon | 2 tablespoons coconut, or |
| 1 teaspoon baking powder | avocado oil |
| ½ teaspoon baking soda | 1 teaspoon pure vanilla extract |

1. Preheat the air fryer to 165ºC. 2. Spray a baking dish lightly with cooking spray. 3. In a medium bowl, mix together all the dry ingredients. 4. In a separate bowl, beat the egg. Add treacle, buttermilk, oil, and vanilla and stir until well mixed. 5. Pour liquid mixture into dry ingredients and stir until well blended. 6. Pour batter into baking dish and bake for 20 minutes, or until toothpick inserted in center of loaf comes out clean.

## Homemade Funnel Cake

**Prep time: 10 minutes | Cook time: 5 minutes | Serves 4**

| | |
|---|---|
| Coconut, or avocado oil, for spraying | 240 ml fat-free vanilla Greek yogurt |
| 110 g self-raising flour, plus more for dusting | ½ teaspoon ground cinnamon |
| | ¼ cup icing sugar |

1. Preheat the air fryer to 190ºC. Line the air fryer basket with baking paper, and spray lightly with oil. 2. In a large bowl, mix together the flour, yogurt and cinnamon until the mixture forms a ball. 3. Place the dough on a lightly floured work surface and knead for about 2 minutes. 4. Cut the dough into 4 equal pieces, then cut each of those into 6 pieces. You should have 24 pieces in total. 5. Roll the pieces into 8- to 10-inch-long ropes. Loosely mound the ropes into 4 piles of 6 ropes. 6. Place the dough piles in the prepared basket, and spray liberally with oil. You may need to work in batches, depending on the size of your air fryer. 7. Cook for 5 minutes, or until lightly browned. 8. Dust with the icing sugar before serving.

## Breaded Bananas with Chocolate Topping

**Prep time: 10 minutes | Cook time: 10 minutes | Serves 6**

| | |
|---|---|
| 40 g cornflour | 3 bananas, halved crosswise |
| 25 g plain breadcrumbs | Cooking spray |
| 1 large egg, beaten | Chocolate sauce, for serving |

1. Preheat the air fryer to175ºC. 2. Place the cornflour, breadcrumbs, and egg in three separate bowls. 3. Roll the bananas in the cornstarch, then in the beaten egg, and finally in the breadcrumbs to coat well. 4. Spritz the air fryer basket with the cooking spray. 5. Arrange the banana halves in the basket and mist them with the cooking spray. Air fry for 5 minutes. Flip the bananas and continue to air fry for another 2 minutes. 6. Remove the bananas from the basket to a serving plate. Serve with the chocolate sauce drizzled over the top.

## Air Fried Mint Pie

**Prep time: 15 minutes | Cook time: 25 minutes | Serves 2**

| | |
|---|---|
| 1 tablespoon instant coffee | 1 teaspoon dried mint |
| 2 tablespoons almond butter, softened | 3 eggs, beaten |
| | 1 teaspoon dried spearmint |
| 2 tablespoons granulated sweetener | 4 teaspoons coconut flour |
| | Cooking spray |

1. Spray the air fryer basket with cooking spray. 2. Then mix all ingredients in the mixer bowl. 3. When you get a smooth mixture, transfer it in the air fryer basket. Flatten it gently. Cook the pie at 185ºC for 25 minutes.

## Chickpea Brownies

**Prep time: 10 minutes | Cook time: 20 minutes | Serves 6**

| | |
|---|---|
| Vegetable oil | cocoa powder |
| 425 g can chickpeas, drained | 1 tablespoon espresso powder |
| and rinsed | (optional) |
| 4 large eggs | 1 teaspoon baking powder |
| 80 ml coconut oil, melted | 1 teaspoon baking soda |
| 80 ml honey | 80 g chocolate chips |
| 3 tablespoons unsweetened | |

1. Preheat the air fryer to 165°C. 2. Generously grease a baking pan with vegetable oil. 3. In a blender or food processor, combine the chickpeas, eggs, coconut oil, honey, cocoa powder, espresso powder (if using), baking powder, and baking soda. Blend or process until smooth. Transfer to the prepared pan and stir in the chocolate chips by hand. 4. Set the pan in the air fryer basket and bake for 20 minutes, or until a toothpick inserted into the center comes out clean. 5. Let cool in the pan on a wire rack for 30 minutes before cutting into squares. 6. Serve immediately.

## Spiced Apple Cake

**Prep time: 15 minutes | Cook time: 30 minutes | Serves 6**

| | |
|---|---|
| Vegetable oil | 1 tablespoon apple pie spice |
| 2 diced & peeled Gala apples | ½ teaspoon ground ginger |
| 1 tablespoon fresh lemon juice | ¼ teaspoon ground cardamom |
| 55 g unsalted butter, softened | ¼ teaspoon ground nutmeg |
| 65 g granulated sugar | ½ teaspoon kosher, or coarse |
| 2 large eggs | sea salt |
| 155 g plain flour | 60 ml whole milk |
| 1½ teaspoons baking powder | Icing sugar, for dusting |

1. Grease a 0.7-liter Bundt, or tube pan with oil; set aside. 2. In a medium bowl, toss the apples with the lemon juice until well coated; set aside. 3. In a large bowl, combine the butter and sugar. Beat with an electric hand mixer on medium speed until the sugar has dissolved. Add the eggs and beat until fluffy. Add the flour, baking powder, apple pie spice, ginger, cardamom, nutmeg, salt, and milk. Mix until the batter is thick but pourable. 4. Pour the batter into the prepared pan. Top batter evenly with the apple mixture. Place the pan in the air fryer basket. Set the air fryer to 175°C and cook for 30 minutes, or until a toothpick inserted in the center of the cake comes out clean. Close the air fryer and let the cake rest for 10 minutes. Turn the cake out onto a wire rack and cool completely. 5. Right before serving, dust the cake with icing sugar.

## Rhubarb and Strawberry Crumble

**Prep time: 10 minutes | Cook time: 12 to 17 minutes | Serves 6**

| | |
|---|---|
| 250 g sliced fresh strawberries | or plain flour |
| 95 g sliced rhubarb | 50 g packed light brown sugar |
| 75 g granulated sugar | ½ teaspoon ground cinnamon |
| 60 g quick-cooking oatmeal | 3 tablespoons unsalted butter, |
| 50 g whole-wheat pastry flour, | melted |

1. Insert the crisper plate into the basket and the basket into the unit. Preheat the unit to 190°C. 2. In a 6-by-2-inch round metal baking pan, combine the strawberries, rhubarb, and granulated sugar. 3. In a medium bowl, stir together the oatmeal, flour, brown sugar, and cinnamon. Stir the melted butter into this mixture until crumbly. Sprinkle the crumble mixture over the fruit. 4. Once the unit is preheated, place the pan into the basket. 5.Bake for 12 minutes then check the crumble. If the fruit is bubbling and the topping is golden brown, it is done. If not, resume cooking. 6. When the cooking is complete, serve warm.

## Baked Brazilian Pineapple

**Prep time: 10 minutes | Cook time: 10 minutes | Serves 4**

| | |
|---|---|
| 95 g brown sugar | cored, and cut into spears |
| 2 teaspoons ground cinnamon | 3 tablespoons unsalted butter, |
| 1 small pineapple, peeled, | melted |

1. In a small bowl, mix the brown sugar and cinnamon until thoroughly combined. 2. Brush the pineapple spears with the melted butter. Sprinkle the cinnamon-sugar over the spears, pressing lightly to ensure it adheres well. 3. Place the spears in the air fryer basket in a single layer. (Depending on the size of your air fryer, you may have to do this in batches.) Set the air fryer to 200°C and cook for 10 minutes for the first batch (6 to 8 minutes for the next batch, as the fryer will be preheated). Halfway through the cooking time, brush the spears with butter. 4. The pineapple spears are done when they are heated through, and the sugar is bubbling. Serve hot.

# Cream-Filled Sponge Cakes

**Prep time: 10 minutes | Cook time: 10 minutes | Makes 4 cakes**

Coconut, or avocado oil, for spraying

1 tube croissant dough

4 cream-filled sponge cake fingers

1 tablespoon icing sugar

1. Line the air fryer basket with baking paper, and spray lightly with oil. 2. Unroll the dough into a single flat layer and cut it into 4 equal pieces. 3. Place 1 sponge cake in the center of each piece of dough. Wrap the dough around the cake, pinching the ends to seal. 4. Place the wrapped cakes in the prepared basket, and spray lightly with oil. 5. Bake at 90°C for 5 minutes, flip, spray with oil, and cook for another 5 minutes, or until golden brown. 6. Dust with the icing sugar and serve.

Printed in Great Britain
by Amazon

16343782R00036